"Help us, Somebody" (Te

*I've seen it on this estate. There was a lady
to her. She was worried stiff because she i
had to move because of problems when they were ....
and the Council promises that they'd move them, this that and the other.
And nothing ever went right. She said that she had fears that the same
thing was going to happen with this - we'll all be waiting and waiting and
waiting - and they found her one morning dead in bed. Now the worry
that played on her mind for over 19 months was tremendous, and it does -
regardless of what they say when they're building these new homes - and
they look lovely, all very well - but if you're looking down the line at three,
four or five years, it's a long time.*

(Pat, Newport)

*We received a letter from the Director of Housing on the 9th July 2003
saying that although the Prefabs are popular all tenants will be moved to
alternative Council accommodation. We hadn't received any form of noti-
fication from the Council for almost twelve months when this letter ar-
rived.. I was so angry.*

*To send a letter like that to the elderly people, it was so, so cruel. I think
they were trying to give some elderly people heart attacks, kill them off out
of the way, it was so callous to send a letter like that. I can't imagine
what the man was thinking about.*

(Dave, Bristol)

*My husband was seriously wounded in the Second World War and over
the years was in different hospitals for more operations. After much suffering he died nine years ago. Now, at 84, I am faced with the stress and
worry of being moved out of my home. It is on my mind all the time. I
feel it's not the Prefabs they are concerned about, it is the land they are on,
and for that we old people have to suffer and our way of life is taken away.*

(Tenant aged 84, Bristol)

'DEATH SENTENCE'

(Banner, Bristol 2003)

"HELP US, SOMEBODY"

THE DEMOLITION OF THE ELDERLY

Bob Dumbleton

First published by The London Press, UK 2006

ISBN: 1-905006-14-4

A C.I.P. reference is available from the British Library.

Printed and bound in Great Britain

CONTENTS

NOTE

I joined the Central Ward of the Cardiff City Labour Party in 1965. It was the time of the slum clearances from the inner city, and of town centre redevelopment with new shops, offices, roads, car parks, leisure amenities.

I became a volunteer housing activist from the Cardiff experience and later advised people in Swansea and Port Talbot when they were resisting demolition. It was a period of intense and widespread 'community action' in England, Wales and Scotland, as town maps were being redrawn. I left the Labour Party to devote my energies to this radical movement.

Later, with the slum clearance programme giving way to 'rehabilitation' schemes for homes and streets, I moved out to the council estates in the towns and valleys of South Wales to support Tenants Action Groups and Tenants and Residents Associations.

This led to the creation of the Welsh Tenants Federation, which links Associations from all over Wales. When I first met the residents of Newport's prefabs in 2000 I was an advisor to the South East Region of the WTF.

All the housing work over these decades has been a collaboration with the people with the problems. I was good for letter writing, at least, I was sometimes told.

I wasn't good for getting across the message written up here: our housing system kills. So here goes again.

1. INTRODUCTION

Forcing elderly and often ill people out of their homes can shorten lives. It can kill them. It is killing them all the time. It happens to people when their houses and their streets are being 're-developed,' 're-generated.' The demolition and replacement of obsolete, unhealthy housing is regarded as necessary and welcome in almost every respect. The 'Urban Renaissance' of the headlines. For some, perhaps most, these changes are a lease of life. For others it is an upheaval too far.

They are not easy deaths. Fear is a cause. Drawn out anxiety aggravates the diseases of age. And people get very tired as the process takes several years.

What people suffer is not seen, the crying not heard. They are hidden in the good news of 're-generation'. They are discounted as the moans and jitters of the old folk.

What is in the minds of those responsible for these plans is one question. And what is in the minds of those who carry them out, people who do see and hear what they are doing, is another.

The evidence produced here is largely from the demolition of the prefab homes in Newport (Gwent) and in Bristol. The Prefabs have a special history, a special architecture and construction. But to take them as a specially isolated example would be another way of not seeing the reality of a national housing policy and practice.[1]

It is hard to prove that forced moves kill people. They are old anyway. Mr. Brown threatened to sue the Newport Council for stress but died within a month. Mabel, aged 93, died shortly after she was interviewed and we recorded her distress. The first person to move into a new bungalow in Newport died within weeks of being handed the keys by the Welsh Minister.

---

[1] Prefabs. See Appendix I

Ken Nicholas looks out on the 40 new bungalows that replace the 59 prefabs on his Newport site. There are nearly half the original population missing. "Mostly dead." His own angina started last year. He knows there's no proof. But he's in no doubt.

Pat Morris predicted that a third of the people would be lost on his site by the time the work was complete.

These two prefab populations, some 800 households, were, are predominantly the elderly, many of great age. Some, like Daisy of Bristol, have lived in their prefab since they were built 57 years ago.[2]

A few frightened old people scattered across several streets, as they were in the 'slum clearance' days, or are now in a 'redevelopment' area, can die perfectly unnoticed. But in the case of the prefabs, even when the old are virtually all of the population, the un-noticing is the same.

We have asked the Welsh Assembly Government repeatedly since 2000, to undertake research. Count the living and the dead. The same request is being made to the English authorities responsible for Bristol. Perhaps it is already known that people do die because of these policies and practices. Asking for proof is barking up the wrong reality.

The great 'Slum Clearances' programmes that re-mapped our towns and cities, ran up to the 1970s. Some 750,000 homes were demolished. 1,232,983 people were moved. [Housing Returns 1945-1970. Gov Publication]

---

[2] Replies to a survey of Bristol prefab residents came from:

09 aged over 90
48 aged 81-90
104 aged 71-80
95 aged 61-70
70 aged 51-60
25 aged 41-50
09 aged 30-40

We have no figures for the numbers of elderly and ill that had to make this move. We know that 123,613 of those moved were single people. It's a fair guess that many of those would be elderly.

I met some of them in Cardiff in the 1960s. Mrs. Murphy was one. Her family had come to Cardiff in the 1840s to build the docks and found the city.

Mrs. Murphy's doorknocker gleamed and her step shone white. Her young neighbours regretted the loss of their town centre pitch but were glad to lose the damp, the cold, the sound of the rats running the rafters every night... Mrs. Murphy never stopped crying. Forty years on, Mabel couldn't stop crying.

"This is my little grounding, my familiarity," said Mrs.Pugsley, a 73-year-old widow, about her prefab home. How many little groundings, familiarities, lives were lost among the moving million?

I sometimes park my car above the spot where Mrs. Murphy lived. In streets nearby where others I knew lived their last agonised years, there are shops, offices, penthouses. Towns change, and the ways of demolishing old people can look as if they have changed. But they are still dying of it.

Pam was persuaded to sell her prefab and move to a new bungalow because it was heavy pressure, and Slum Clearance was family history. "Compulsory Purchase was always at the back of my mind. My parents were Compulsory Purchased from the Pill area. They got a pittance and my mother died within the year. She loved the place. It belonged to the family she loved. She had a massive heart attack at 68. It happened when she was trying to get her key into the door of the new flat. The place was soulless for her."

Did Pam think that her mother's death was caused by the loss of her home? "Yes, definitely. I know it was."

Some people, elderly and infirm as others, survive happily the years of upheaval with a new home to look forward to. Perhaps a majority in the Newport example.

(A Satisfaction Survey will not count the dead…)

I asked one burly little old gent how he felt about the news of yet another six months delay before he could move into his new home. "O be buggered!" he said, waving it all away. "As long as I've a roof over my head."

O, if we were all like that!

"It depends whether you see the glass half full or half empty," the Director of the scheme at Newport had a way of saying. Against our pleas for those made ill, he could cite the case of Mrs. McDonald: *"I … have been living in my prefab for 56 years. My prefab is not now in good condition … water coming in … rusted panels … draughts cut my legs off. I have not been in good health myself. I suffered a mini stroke a while ago."*

The 'glass half full' analogy reveals an attitude. To save the McDonaldses we lose the Mabels. It's a glib outlook, handy for its deal of overlooking. But I have to remember myself when young. Even as I encountered the Mrs. Murphys and others equally tragic, I had in my head the socialist conviction that the only trouble with Slum Clearance was the too little, too late. We were settling, long overdue, with the 'Housing Inferno' of the Industrial Revolution. There was a deal of overlooking in that view. You could believe that whingeing came with age. That these people would get over it in their new homes. Or you could, confused, just go with the flow.

What we make of what we see and hear is conditioned for us. Denials go with the flow. The distress of seeing distress can be made to go away. 'They'll get over it.'

I am told cheers go up in the local Housing Office when another Bristol prefab resident is winkled out. Our campaigning may have provoked such responses. We have been harshly critical of officials. But perhaps there is, underground, real dislike for age and vulnerability. This isn't just a hell of good intentions. "Absolute hell" was scrawled across a survey form from Newport. "Nightmare", "Torture", "Torment", are the words of George (91) and Jenny (72) for their experiences.

The penny dropped for me some years after my involvement in Cardiff, Swansea, Port Talbot clearances. When my elderly mother became very agitated, when we insisted on necessary work to her house, I saw the shock of change could kill people. We had killed people, lots and lots of them.

It is not easy, in the middle of a 'Regeneration' scheme, to go round saying this is killing people. It is not kind, when there is so much fear anyway. You want to get people through it. And the media shy away from the fact, on their own account.

I got it into my head that I was the only man on the island who knew this method of ending lives had happened, and was happening. I saw Mrs. Murphy in 1966 and Mabel in 2002.

A barrage of letters, a videotape, interview transcripts, were aimed at the Welsh Assembly from 2000 onwards. I was escorted by police from one Housing Committee. None of this had any effect.

In the summer of 2003 Bristol's Prefab people demonstrated at a Council meeting. The first banner to catch the eye was inscribed with the words "DEATH SENTENCE." The word was out. News about the old on their remote planet takes decades to arrive.

We haven't jumped from Slum Clearance to Prefab Replacement. Some 40,000 homes were demolished in the 1990s. No figures are available for the elderly and ill amongst them. No news about those dying to stay put.

In the coming decade the Government's 'Pathfinder' programme to regenerate towns in Northern England will demolish tens of thousands of homes.

2. METHOD

The evidence that the old and ill can be upset to death when their homes are demolished is presented through people's own words.

I became an advisor to the Newport Prefab Residents Association in 2001 when the 'regeneration' plan had been approved. I had been active in various housing issues back to the slum clearance era of the 1960s and 70s. The PRA was a group of tenants and prefab owners critical of all or some aspects of the scheme.

Other Residents Associations founded by the landlord, Newport Housing Trust, supported the plan, looked forward to the new homes.

I have been active with the Newport residents, opposing or critical of what was happening to them. I blotted my copybook with Newport Housing Trust, the agents of change, and holders of information, early on. The Welsh Assembly Government stone walled all my badgering for 'proper' research - i.e. examination of the mortality rates. My application, under the Freedom of Information Act, for the number of deaths at Newport, the raw data to think about, and perhaps compare, has just been turned down.

Letters from the Welsh Assembly Government in reply to mine invariably said, in effect, 'Go away, all is fine.' Letters to Newport Council and the Housing Trust went unanswered. Particularly frustrating was the failure to get any reply from the Health Ministry at WAG. Letters addressed to the medical people were automatically re-directed to the Housing Department for reply.

We coaxed some comments from medical persons. Some we approached were cagey about political involvement. Some made the scientific point that with several possible causes of death in the old and ill, one cause could not be proved. Others said what needs to be said. And some of these conveyed that whatever they said on such an issue, the powers that be would take no notice. Which has been the case.

No one is writing 'Demolition' as a cause of death on a Death Certificate. And no one wants to initiate scientific enquiries or undertake research.[3]

'Evidence-based policies' are a key piece of Government rhetoric. But then someone can decide not to collect the evidence. The people's voices collected here are in that diminished and dismissible category of evidence, 'anecdotal'.

No politician or official ever met the argument that people died because they were being 'regenerated'. Blankness was all.

How can these things be? The suffering is visible enough. The voices are audible enough. If the planners and politicians are out of sight and earshot, the imagining is not so difficult. It is a cliché of our time, the trauma of home moving. Apply that to the elderly, and make it a forced move, and what have you got?

And how can so little have been learnt since 'slum' clearing? And why didn't we know what a wipe-out that was?

These mysteries are tackled in Section Five: 'Theories of Not-Caring'.

I am recalling slum clearance experiences from the 1960s and 70s in Cardiff and Swansea. And there's evidence from recent local clearances, at Penarth, Vale of Glamorgan, Glyntaff, Pontypridd (a 'refurbishment') and Chapel Hillside, Rhondda.

Most voices here are from the Newport and Bristol prefab sites. They offer the special example of a concentrated population of mainly elderly people. These very different 'regeneration' schemes came to more or less the same results. The more or less dying result. I can provide only stories, not statistics.

---

[3] Or no one is prepared to fund such research.

The Government's 'Pathfinder' programme licenses large clearances across 'derelict' areas of English northern towns. The good intentions stand out a mile. Blighted areas of housing and former industrial land will be re-developed by the 'partners', elected councils and private enterprise. The scale of demolition has aroused strong opposition because the run-down streets also contain perfectly fit, or remediable, homes. It is not clear if elderly persons are among the protesters. They tend to go, one way or another, quietly.

In 2005 a select committee of Parliament investigated the 'Pathfinder' programme. In its report to the Housing Minister (Deputy Prime Minister John Prescott) there is the call for more 'consultation' with residents. Without more consultation, the report says the Pathfinders will 'repeat the mistakes' of previous clearance programmes.' What, after so many decades of clearing, are the mistakes reckoned to be? What are the lessons Parliamentarians have learnt?

These investigators conclude that the 'heritage of areas may be destroyed' and that they may be 'replaced with neighbourhoods of little lasting value.'

The select MPs don't know the lasting value of the lives being destroyed? "They pity the plumage and forget the dying bird."

I'm safe, I think, in saying my time with the Prefab Residents Association has made me some very good friends. And the time of this growing friendship shows me people frightened at the prospect of great change, the extreme anxiety of 'decanting' and moving, and the painful difficulties, and even impossibilities, of 'settling down' in the new home. It's not over when it's over. Witness Moira, Mary, Peggy...

3. THE PLAN

Newport

News of the plans for the Newport Prefabs began to reach residents after 1998. Work began in 2000/2001. The last phase is now in progress. Some 360 prefabs on five main sites in the town are being demolished. They are being replaced by purpose-built bungalows. Some hundred prefabs had been bought by their tenants.

Prefab owners have choices. They can take on a new bungalow under the 'Homebuy' scheme. The Welsh Assembly Government provides an interest free loan. The loan is then repaid when the property is sold, or the owner dies. Owners can buy a bungalow from their own resources or they can become tenants of the new landlord. In all cases owners receive 'market value' for their former homes, as decided by the District valuer.

A handful of owners have chosen to remain in their prefabs. They have been, and are being, built around. Other owners say they would have done the same, if they had known this was an option. They moved because they feared Compulsory Purchase. Tenants do not have the choice to stay. Any resistance is met with threats of eviction (Chris and Carol) or of being put on the Council waiting list for a move elsewhere (Peggy).

Efforts were made to give the most disabled only one move, from prefab to new bungalow. Others faced months of 'decanting' into mobile homes sited nearby.

The project is being carried out by Newport Housing Trust. The prefabs were transferred to this not-for-profit landlord after a ballot of tenants. This 'stock-transfer' meant funds could be borrowed to carry out the scheme. (Newport Council itself has limited financial resources under government rules.) A large majority of tenants voted for the scheme. The choice was posed between having new 'show-place' bungalows, and accelerated decline of their prefab homes.

This plan kept the 'community' together. The new bungalows were built on the prefab sites. It catered for the motor car. Each car owner can park on the home patch. Also providing direct access for ambulances, fire engines, etc. Little wonder over 90% of tenants voted for the transfer to Newport Housing Trust, and the move. People had voted for what they got. Any criticism of the plan and its implementation met that powerful reply.

The bungalows are lovely but you get brain-damaged on the way.
(Bill Eben)

The worst is, I sit here and don't know what to do. Sometimes I really feel I want to smash the place up.
(Mary Thomas, over a year in her new bungalow)

The bungalow is lovely. We are very happy here. No complaints about anything.
(Survey answer)

David Ford February 2002

This report is based on experiences over the last 20 months since the announcement by Newport Borough Council that there was no long term future for the prefabs and that any prefab that becomes empty will be demolished. It is also the experiences my wife and I have had over the last 39 years and 17 years respectively, as my wife was born in the Treberth Estate and her parents still live there after 48 years.

To fully understand the direct consequences it had on a great many residents both psychologically and physically, you need to look at the nature of the communities and the sequence and timescale of Newport Borough Council policy decisions, as well as consultation procedures.

There is no denying that something had to be done about many of the Council owned properties as they were in a state of disrepair and neglect, exposing Newport Borough Council to tenants' 'right to repair' and 'right to improvement' claims. However, it must also be stated that virtually all the privately owned properties were in a high state of repair, as were a number of tenanted prefabs where the tenants had modernised their properties.

Many residents, both tenants and owners, felt they had no option but to agree to Newport Borough Council's proposals for 'New Bungalow' due to the alternative declaration that NBC will continue their demolition programme due to lack of finance to upgrade. This had an effect of producing widespread despondency among the residents. The most common reply I have heard is, "What choice have we got? You can't wind against the Corporation - they'll get what they want and sell off the land, and if I'm still around I'll get a new bungalow."

People involved with the elderly and disabled residents on these estates have noticed a worrying decline in their well-being. When talking to local GPs in the Ringland and Beechwood surgeries, they tell of an increase of residents visiting for treatment. People I have spoken to from the Home Help services have told of the worry these residents have over the future of their homes and the adverse effects it has on their health. Even the toll of deaths has increased since April 1998 on these estates.

My Father in Law, who is aged 78, has mentally and physically aged ten years since April 1998, due to the worry for his future, and that is not an isolated case. Many of the residents I have known and got to know, have been affected in this way. Many feel that being moved at this stage in their lives will literally kill them, and although many have severe health problems they have to date coped, thanks to the fact that they feel secure in their own familiar homes and surroundings.

By far the largest cause of the deterioration of health and well-being is Newport Borough Council's lack of meaningful, clear and sympathetic consultation, and their demolition policy that has ripped out the soul of these communities.

Bristol

Bristol's prefabs residents have had three plans made for them. In the 1990s, Plan A allowed tenants to stay in their own homes, if they wished: "The important point to stress is that you do not have to move out of your prefab if you don't want to." This was the promise to prefab tenants, underlined, in the Bristol tenants' newsletter. [4]

Tenants who wanted to move to new homes were offered pre-fabricated bungalows, 'like for like', built close to their existing homes. Some 400 tenants moved to these new houses, with minimum delays. It was piecemeal planning, based on individual needs.

In the summer of 2003, Bristol Council decided, for financial reasons, that this approach could not be sustained. The remaining 400 prefabs, on some nine sites, would be demolished. Tenants would be rehoused as from the Council Waiting List - that is, anywhere around the city. Owners of their prefabs would also lose their homes, as developers moved into the sites. With 'market value' compensation, they would fend for themselves. This U-turn was announced in a brief letter to the residents from the Council's Director of Housing.

Dave Drew

"The Council announced its plan for us. "We're going to work with the Developers, and you can move off your prefab sites. If some of the sites, when they are developed, contain Council units, you may be able to return." Now to put this to elderly people is just incredible. Incredible that they should even think about addressing people like this. A few of us met in the

---

[4] See Appendix 2.

streets. We could see how upset people were, the stress for elderly people, and the disabled in particular. We decided to go around with a petition and we formed the Prefab preservation Group.

What made me fight the Council's callous decision was when I knocked on a lady's door. She was obviously elderly, she lived on her own. She had lost her husband a few years ago. She had all her faculties and she had kept up with what the newspapers were saying and she had attended the Council's meeting in July. I was very careful talking to her because you have to be with the elderly when you are talking about their homes. but she was actually in tears when she came to the door. She was crying and saying to me, "What are you going to do?" She was just in a terrible state about what was going to happen to her home and I thought this is 2003. Councils or anybody should not be allowed to treat people like this. That's what made me get together with others to form the PPG. Perhaps it should be called the People Preservation Group."

The campaign compiled a survey based on some 400 questionnaire replies from prefab residents. The report of the survey's findings had the title, Help Us, Somebody. Many of the quotations here are taken from comments made to this questionnaire.

After a year of fierce campaigning by the Bristol Prefab Preservation Group, the council was pushed into producing Plan C. Plan C is a 'partnership' between Bristol Council and a private developer. In 2004 Bovis was chosen as partner. The first proposal on which Bovis was chosen was to build 330 new bungalows on existing prefab sites. Bovis, in return, could build 310 homes and flats to sell. A few months later, these figures change: Bovis can build 560 houses and flats to sell, with the bungalows.

Some owners may now stay in their prefab homes. Others, under threat of compulsory purchase, will have to go. Tenants, under threat of eviction, would have to lose their prefab homes. But it looks as if they have won back 'like-for-like'.

I am writing in the lull before the site details of Plan C are finalised. Some owners are determined to resist still.

People are having to re-live their anxieties. Others are dying. The clearing and re-building will take several years. Residents on one site have been told to "go away and not think about it for four years."

It takes a certain type of person to watch others gradually fail. May their consciences be as clear as ours.
(Owner)

It's disgusting the attitude the Council is taking. No regard for old, disabled, lonely people. It's a wonder they can sleep at night.
(Owner, 81)

I am disgusted the way the Council are treating us [OAPs]. I am being treated for stress caused by this you have imposed on us. I would not treat a dog like this. I hope you can sleep at night because I cannot.
(Tenant, 70)

Newport and Bristol

These plans to demolish prefabs are set up differently. The Newport scheme is carried out by a Registered Social Landlord taking over from Newport Council. Bristol Council retains ownership of its tenanted properties with a 'partner', Bovis, carrying out the development.

Newport Housing Trust raises the finance on the private market and through land sales. Bovis builds bungalows for the Council in return for building and selling houses and flats on former Council owned land. In these variations of public/private partnerships the democratic element is maintained. Newport Housing Trust has five councillors and five elected tenants on its Board, alongside five 'independents'. Bovis deals directly with Bristol Council's Housing Department.

Different approaches can bring about the same results. Publicly run or privately funded clearances can create the same consequences. Economic pressures, or the same mentalities, work to the same endings. [5]

---

[5] The brand new National Assembly of Wales invited 'activists' to give evidence to the Working Parties on Housing Policy. I set out my warning about the forthcoming Newport scheme based on my slum clearing experiences. The banker present was the most sympathetically shocked. He had no idea.

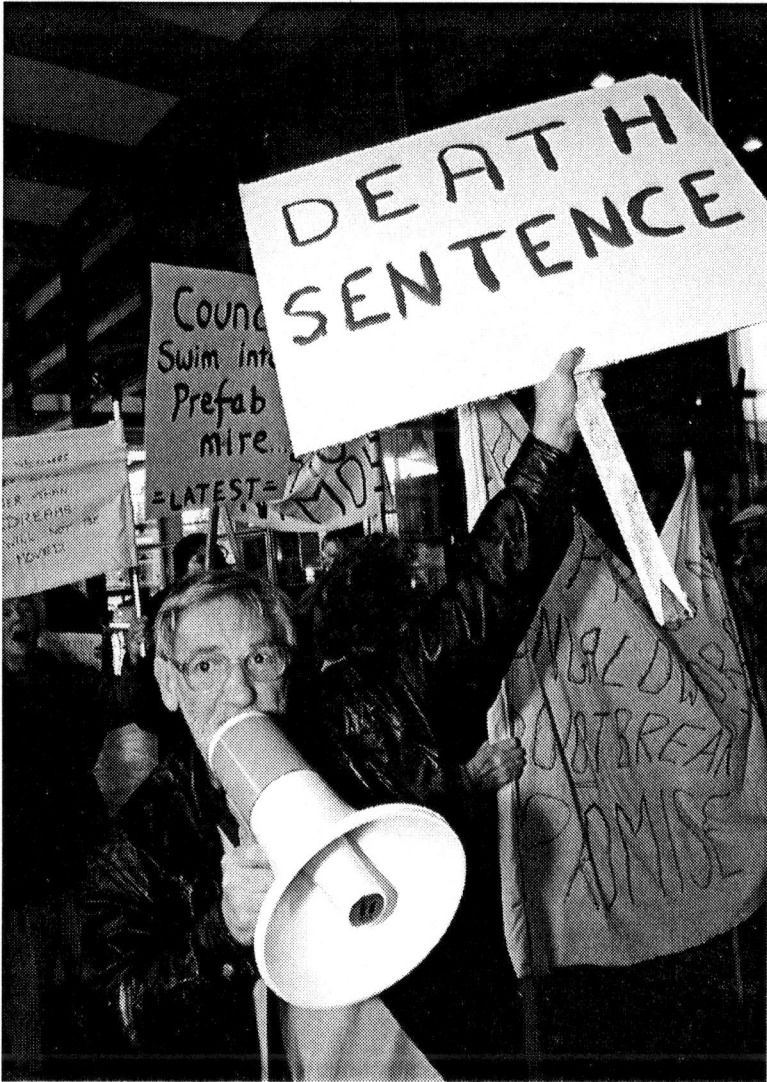

(Photo: Courtesy Bristol United Press)

The residents demonstrate, October 2003. This man had his mother in mind.

SECTION ONE

EVIDENCE

You can't prove it to these people. There will never be evidence enough for them.

(Pam, Newport)

We don't believe a word they say. And they don't believe a word we say.
(Dave Drew, Bristol)

They never showed any sign throughout it all that they knew they were dealing with old people.

(Ken, Newport)

GOING QUIETLY

Why are people so afraid? The war's been over for fifty years.
(Audrey)

I have lived in Shirehampton all my life, having been born here! On this very spot where these few prefabs stand was an orchard we used to play in as children. I love this area. And I do not want to be anywhere else. This is my home, and I pray it will be for many more years.
(Owner, 81)

I cannot think of the possibility of going to live elsewhere. I am so sad and miserable. I pray God will help us to overcome this awful situation.
(Tenant, 69)

My husband prays to God to get us out of all this. He thinks He will, but I doubt it.
(Owners, Newport)

(Bill had probably prayed the same prayer when he was dodging the bullets under the Rhine bridge.)

Daren't comment.
(Tenant, 92)

Pat Morris (Newport)

" There are several examples. You only have to look at people's faces and talk to people. Nobody is going to these people. If they go to a meeting, they sit quiet. You can spot them at a meeting - they don't open their mouths, they are so frightened of speaking in case someone tells them they are wrong - you won't have a new home or you won't have this. It's all the worry and all the stress that they have got on it. These people are nice people, but they are frightened to speak out and say what's really happening to them inside. They need more help than that's been given. These are people who don't want to argue or offend anybody.

There is another chap - he's in a new home. Now no one was going to him, and they found him twice on the floor in his home. But nobody says anything. The lady that is going to come out to one of these new bungalows is eighty years old. They are not looking at the fact that they are going to be putting her from somewhere she's been going around a little room and a kitchen that she's used to, and stick her in something like this. It's going to be nerve racking. They're going to hear the creaks of these new radiators and they'll wonder what it is. Nobody's given any thought to this. It's like taking a goldfish out of a bowl and putting it in a dog basket, saying get on with life. Well what's it going to do? - it's just going to flounder. And elderly people will flounder. They just don't think of that, they're not interested.

There's another lady - she's in a wheelchair - she's a bit astounded at where they've put her - right around the corner, where she can't see anybody or anything. You know, they haven't given consideration to these things because of how closed in she is, she was in a block before where she knew everyone and could talk to her neighbours. "

Jacqui Handley

Jacqui Handley saw what was happening at Newport more than most. She was Chairperson of one of the Residents' groups - the Prefab Residents' Association. She visited all the sites taking up individual problems. Jacqui's mother was a long-term prefab resident. She receives full-time care for her dementia.

" There has been damage to people's lives. Just the factor alone that people have been put into situations they can't control has brought about a lot of stress and anxiety. Some of them have been on medication prior to this, and I think this has exacerbated the situation and people are attending doctors to have increased medication.

It's a worry where people don't attend doctors but who are

suffering these things, and they are maybe the people who have suffered the most in all of this. People who haven't been talking to people. People who haven't really known what was going on. I think they would be the slightly older generation. People able to get involved in groups would do better. There are always a certain percentage not able to access information and don't go to doctors or have family support, wouldn't be telling the doctors...

I am sure it's shortened a lot of people's lives. I know from the way it's made me feel, and the stresses I've had to deal with. Some of these people I just don't know - I'm half their age - I try to imagine the impact it had on them. It's had a big impact on my life, and I'm a little on the outside because I'm dealing with my mother, and my mother doesn't have the awareness that a lot of people have.

What affected people in their day-in day-out living, was the fact that they couldn't really know what was happening to them. The scheme didn't allow for a lot of information unless you were actually being decanted, or if you were in the phase to be moved next. "We are not talking to you yet," was what people were told. That made the situation a lot worse.

In the early stages a lot of information was going out, letters and whatever, but it was never very informative. It never said, "We'll do this" - and when, and how. Lots of things came through the door. Some people just didn't understand that there had been a transfer of landlord, really. They thought the vote was voting for a new home. There'd be rumours. They'd know their home was involved in all this, but the detail - what it meant for them - that uncertainty caused a lot of stress and anxiety. In the early days there were no Resident Liaison Officers. There was not the number of staff on board to even cope with people accessing information. In the early days that was very poor. There should have been more people on board. More people for people. Not people for building homes. People for people.

People were vulnerable. People have sold their homes [to the Trust] and now they feel that wasn't the right thing to do. They were told certain things which influenced their decision. There are regrets. Some poor souls - not all, but some...

I always remember one meeting - you were there and carrying a briefcase, you looked a bit more official - and people were frightened to say what they were really feeling. I remember going to one house where they had problems with the floor, and I was told on no account was I to say anything to the Trust, and that left me in a real dilemma. If the couple had an accident, I would feel responsible, but I was never allowed to say anything.

I don't know all the details of why [there was such fear]. I think they thought that if they complained it would alter their prospects [to have the move of their choice]. They might make them move off the estate.

I've learnt a lot myself, really - learnt to look at things differently, and especially with elderly people.

You know, you look and think they're fine - but underneath they're very good at hiding things. They have been so used to a system whereby they are told what is expected. They were grateful for what they got after the war when these homes were provided. They were always used to a system when if you were on the Council waiting list, they were told, "This is what you do," and what have you. A lot found this process very difficult.

I've learnt an awful lot about old people. You know, we have taken complaints forward, but most people don't like to complain. It's an area I'm most concerned about, of people who don't complain. people that suffer... People like the woman who had a bad heart, who carried buckets of water from the kitchen sink, because she couldn't get the toilet to work. And she shouldn't have been doing it. The repair hadn't been done, and they hadn't been made aware of it...

Elderly people like routine - like to know what they are doing and why they are doing it. Like to have their meals at certain times, like to set out and plan, and get on with their life day-to-day. All these interruptions, all these people coming in and out, all these new faces - they just found it so hard to cope with. They would speak to people [from the Trust] and you'd ask them, "Who did you speak to?" and they'd say, "We don't know" - they really weren't sure who it was. Or someone would come in, and they'd feel they had been made a promise, but they didn't know who it was, or they couldn't remember....

I think some were in turmoil. I can't imagine how it must have been... And they were very trusting. I found that very difficult. If someone gives them information, they trust that person to be telling them the truth. I don't know why that is. Especially official people coming in. I felt a lot of people were very vulnerable. There were big decisions about their homes, about their lives, and they didn't always have somebody there who could say, "Hang on - what about this, what about that?" - so really they had to take it, whether they were happy with it or not.

They were the people who couldn't cope with getting into the situation where they said, "No, I'm not really happy with that." Official people come into your home and you have to say "Yes." You have to be grateful. I think that some of them would have been far happier if they'd been left alone.

I blame the Welsh Assembly. They could have done more. This was a unique situation. A stock transfer. A redevelopment. And a population of vulnerable people. Their Health people did nothing.

There were lots and lots of nights I couldn't get to sleep. Exhaustion was one thing, having to do too much... the problems people had. Worry that you'd done enough. Worry about what you could do. Worry about the impact on people. Worry about the way sites were left. Worry there'd be a phone call saying someone had had an accident. So many different things.

The vulnerability ... people living on their own...”

George (91) and Jenny (72) moved three times. They were asked to help the Trust and a disabled couple. So they vacated the prefab they had been decanted to, and went into a mobile home. "A glorified caravan."

"It nearly killed me," says George. "I thought I was handing in my chips." He developed angina. "It was all right for two weeks at the seaside, but not for eight months through the winter." The banquette seating was "torture". It was cold. They had rats, and a burglary.

Pam hid her feelings, through the years of upheaval. She was nervous about being interviewed. So much had been bottled up. She had "shut herself off." She sold her prefab home to the Trust.

They sat in my conservatory, four men, and made these promises. I'd have the same garden and the same size bungalow. It would be new and beautiful... The architect said he would like to "transpose his ideas" into my head, so I could see how much I would like it.... I was compliant. I believed their promises. I thought I had to do this.

So Pam's "nightmare" began. In her new bungalow for twelve months, she realises what she has lost. Privacy and amenity, some land and light - easy relations with her neighbours. Work is still outstanding. Some possessions are in store... "People look at your new home and say, "Isn't it lovely."

One day I lost it completely, and my friend said she thought the men in the white coats would come for me. I was prescribed Diazapam. My sleep problems have got worse. I'm in limbo. Talking to people now, because I hid it - pride comes into it - I realise how much effect it had on me. I was a coper. I had to cope. Now I'm always doing this. [Pam is nearly crying.] It's worse than bereavement.

Pam's husband died suddenly, fifteen years ago. They had lost a young son. In recent years, close family members have also died from accident and illness. How can this upheaval and change of home be compared to a bereavement? "With bereavement, you know where you are." This is the way Pam (and others) explain it. You know where the pain is coming from. Destroying as the pain is, you can hope emotions will change or end. With all this, you "don't know where you are." It seems that the drastic removal from the home and settled way of life for 33 years is a special form of mental and emotional stress. Knowing where you are is knowing who you are. In Pam's case, also, this was another "bereavement" on top of too many others.

Grieving for a person is recognised, and respected. The story Pam is telling of her last four years, is of her disrespectful treatment. Pam's sense of being 'in limbo' - out of kilter with others, and with her own life - continues in the new bungalow.

Mrs. B.

Mrs. B. was in her late eighties, maybe even 90. This story is told by neighbours. For the last three to four years in her prefab, she had been going blind. She had one son, who visited regularly. Her neighbours shopped for her, and popped in regularly. She didn't take much notice of the plans to demolish the prefab, at first. "She probably thought she wouldn't still be here when it came to it."

When it came to it, she got agitated, very agitated. She couldn't read, or see the TV, or see much at all - but she wanted to be independent... She was very scared of falling.

In the new bungalow, the neighbours kept up their visits and help. "I thought they'd put up handrails for you?" they asked her. Handrails in the hallway, to get around on, had been booked. But there were no handrails when Mrs. B. fell and broke a hip.

That was in September or October. The neighbours visited her in hospital with a Christmas present. Mrs. B. died shortly after. "If she had belonged to me," said one of the neighbours, "I would have gone apeshit."

From Newport

They intimidate you.

(Mary Thomas)

They make you feel you don't exist.

(Penny Hiscocks)

"They talked down to us."
"They looked down on us."
"They were unfeeling."
"We were treated like children."

(Jenny and George Burrows)

I could take you to two people. One is really stressed out over the strain of not getting things done. He's lost a bit of weight, and seems to be going downhill. He's been moved into a bungalow on the main road, and people walking by can see straight in. It floods there, as well, and they keep saying, they're going to do this, they're going to do something. When I told him he was moving into that one, he said, "I don't like that - I don't want to move in there." They said, "You've got a choice - you either move in there, or you leave the estate." Now that, to me, is totally wrong."

(Pat Morris)

[Peggy] had a gun pointed to her head - told if she wouldn't move into that place, she'd be put on the [Council] Waiting List. They didn't say that at the beginning. Compassion or decency, didn't have any of that.

(John Ferris)

From Bristol

My prefab is all I've got in my life. (85)

Being disabled, my current home caters for all my needs and to move would be more than I could bear. (82)

We don't want to leave here, because we are very happy here. (91)

My husband is a very sick man - he could do without all this worry.
(Resident of 50 years.)

I am disabled. I live on my own. I have home care every day. Why move us? We have to change doctors, chemists, post offices - and why do they want to move us at our age? I know a couple of women - one is ninety-two - and one said to me, "I hope I die before it happens."
(Tenant)

I've attended meetings where there's been a lot of elderly people. I just couldn't believe what Council officials were saying to these elderly people. I'm talking about 70- and 90-year-olds. They were being told they had got to move off their prefab sites. They didn't know where to, or how long it would take to find something suitable. And people would be evicted if they didn't move. I just couldn't believe it. I actually recorded some of it on tape. One lady phoned me one day, she was crying. She had a Council officer in her home, telling her to fill out a Transfer Application. If she didn't, she would be evicted. That was a lady in her late 70s and she was actually crying over the phone. It's unbelievable. It leaves me speechless.
(Dave Drew, Bristol)

Billy Banks Estate, Penarth

January 1970, my children and I moved into a brand new maisonette. Our landlord was the local Council. It's now January 2000. The maisonette is still my home. I've wonderful views. There are shops, schools, pub, bus stops and a train station very close.

But not many people wanted to stay here - people only saw it as a place to stop for a short while. The estates gained a bad reputation - tenants felt as if they were being blamed for any criminal activity that took place. They wanted to move. So when regeneration of the area was announced in 1997, I thought that all the tenants would be pleased. Most of them weren't. Moving because you wanted to was one thing, but having to was another matter.

A lot of people thought they were being moved away to make room for people with money, as we were living on a prime site. There were also fears that the landlord could force them to move anywhere in the Vale, and many people had always lived in Penarth. Even though every tenant was visited by a housing officer, because there were no concrete plans people were very fearful, and believed there were plans they weren't being told about [planning behind closed doors]. Then there were the rumours. There was going to be a hotel, a golf course, a road. Cardiff Bay had bought the land - we all had to move out in March, before Christmas, in the New Year, and so on. And I've lost count of the times I spoke to people who have "seen the plans".

(Shirley Sansom)

Chapel Hillside, Rhondda

Part of a 1960s estate, Chapel Hillside is, like the Billy Banks at Penarth, heavily stigmatised. The residents are of mixed ages. There was a long running down, as the Council changed its mind and plans several times. Some people had three moves.

Dilwyn Bishop described serious medical conditions that arose during this period, including strokes, depression, anxiety. He reports increased drinking, and family conflicts... "People became so angry. They were inclined to blame each other."

As houses got boarded up, vandalism, fires and break-ins were rife. And yet Dilwyn reports people's anger at being made to move. "Over my dead body," several said. "Why does it happen like this?" I asked Dilwyn. "Because they treat housing as units, and not people's homes," he said.

Some people go more quietly than others. If there were more like this:

They should leave well alone. Tenants should block traffic on main roads. They only listen when you fight back and cause disruption and bring attention to the problem. Enough residents on a pedestrian crossing for one hour would make them think.

(Owner aged 92, Bristol)

Or this:

I went to my doctor some four months ago, and told him of my symptoms. I also advised everyone else affected to do the same. People will realise when it is too late to go on record. My doctor's advice was that this is democracy at work, and to keep on pressing the buttons and not take it personally. How the bloody hell can you do that?

(Tenant, 72)

Almost all do go quietly in the end. The protest actions and groups usually involve a minority. They are easily headed off, divided, or simply ignored. Still, being part of them is to experience the friendship of resourceful people, and the potential for a different democracy.

Some people couldn't comment, express their hopes and fears. The going quietly can be seen in how they look, the tired eyes, the anxious looks between wives and husbands - hands pressed to heads, sorts of smile, and little jokes.

"He was shaking. He's 92, and he was shaking all over. His wife said it was because they were moving in a couple of days." When Jack Denman told me that about his neighbour, I recalled knocking on a condemned door 40 years before.

A woman came with coal black on her face. She had said, "I lie awake at night, and though I'm warm, I'm shivering."

After a public meeting at Newport's Gaer site I asked an elderly couple how they felt. Perhaps because of my accent, or because I carried papers, or because they were too full to talk to anyone, they turned tail. They clutched hands and turned away as fast as they were able. It was almost comical, had it not been so shaming. Then, and now as I write it.

HEALTH

From the conversation I've had with them, I don't think the Trust necessarily see that their obligation in all this is the health impact. Their priority is the business issues. they are separate issues in their minds. I won't say they are totally irresponsible, but I think from the business side of things there were only so many fact ors they were able to deal with, and those had to be priority.

(Jacqui Handley, Newport)

Everybody admits that moving house is very stressful. People move homes for a job or for more space - to be nearer a school. But when you come to a forced move for somebody in their 70s or 80s - a forced move away from a community they've lived in for decades - the stress involved is unbelievable.

Nobody in their right minds can say anything different. But these Council officers turn a complete blind eye to it. They don't want to know. They say they must do this because otherwise the Housing Revenue budget and business plan won't balance. Everything revolves around money but the human side is ignored completely.

I honestly think all this is going to shorten people's lives. It is just too much for elderly people to be faced with a forced move. It's too much for them to take.

You just can't imagine the stress. One of my neighbours, aged 79, was born in this area, and she's just full of dread at the thought of moving away from Ashton Vale.   (Dave Drew, Bristol)

Janet doubts whether she would have bought the prefab, had she known of this plan. "I bought because I couldn't afford to rent. I took out a Retirement mortgage as the best way out for me." Asked about her mobility and health problems, Janet laughs. "Do you want to be here until Christmas?" She has spinal problems: "The spine is crumbling - it's called spinal sterosis" - heart and blood problems. The most worry at the moment is the aorta valve." She also has angina and hiatus hernia. "I could go on ...."

Does Janet think that her worries about the finances, about the move, have an effect on her health? "I think so, because the aorta valve has happened in the last two years, and that's to do with all this stress and everything.... Yes, it's very stressful. I get bouts when I can't walk and I'm in bed for six weeks at a time. And it's the stress factor."

A few hours after this interview, Janet was taken to hospital with a suspected heart attack. She was discharged two days later with the diagnosis of a severe attack of angina.

From Newport (A small survey on two sites)

Hell on earth since 2000.   (A couple, 70 + and 80 + re-spectively)

Panic attacks.   (80 +)

We even had to cancel a holiday because my blood pressure was too high. I feel it was stress caused this.

Worried from Day One. Had so many callers from the Trust - very little resolved.

I had a stroke in November 2003, caused by the worry of it all.
                    (70 +)

Because of the worry I've had two attacks of vertigo. I do take blood pres-sure tablets, but these don't stop the attacks, because of the worry.
                    (Tenant, 70+)

This survey contained some very positive comments about the Trust and the new properties - but also this:

My chest has been really bad due to dust and fibreglass and asbestos, because of the way the prefabs are being pulled down (no warning of this) ... The dust is causing me to have trouble breathing. I have been hospitalised twice due to chemicals and dust in the demolition of prefabs. I do not think in any way the NHT [Newport Housing Trust] has been co-operative in this Project, and I am taking my complaint further. (70+)

The asbestos story is a bit of a mystery. When previously Newport Council demolished prefabs as they became vacant, full asbestos precautions were taken. None of this happens when the Trust demolishes. The JCBs smash the properties down. It's obviously cheaper. The Health and Safety Executive are satisfied. If you believe them, the gentleman quoted above has nothing to worry about.

(In Bristol, when demolishing prefabs some precautions are taken when removing the external panels. Then the JCBs move in.)

From the Bristol Survey [6]

My husband is a very sick man. He could do without all this worry.
(Owner, resident for 50 years)

My health has deteriorated in the last two years. The worry and stress caused by losing my home has made it a great deal worse.
(Owner, resident for 50 years)

I am recovering from a life threatening illness which has caused depression. My depression is now worse. I am worried about my elderly mum who

---

[6] Survey forms (see Appendix 3) were sent out to 402 prefab addresses (300 tenants and 102 homeowners). Tenants returned 293 forms from 270 households. Homeowners returned 98 forms from 82 households. Some 274 comments were made on the forms. Of these, 10 supported the idea of a move.

lives in a Prefab.

(Tenant, 54)

I have a very rare disease. I am disgusted the way myself and other tenants are being treated. The Council only think of themselves. I am 37 years old. I am severely disabled.

(Tenant of seven months)

Been in hospital three times with heart trouble this year. Going to have a scan. Myocardial Perfusion suspected. My own view, stress. Myself I think it's all over this Council problem.

(Tenant, 67)

I am being treated for cancer, which is very stressful, so this is not helping my condition.

(This person has had a series of strokes, is bedridden, and is not aware of what is happening.)

I have a new bungalow with solid foundations, which took four months to build. How can they justify to want to knock it down? Simply to put more on my land - and they say they won't make a profit. It's pure and simple greed. We were given the right to buy, so in God's name who has the right to take it away? Thank you and others for what you are doing. My dear husband has leukaemia so the stress is hard enough already. I'm trying to keep my fighting spirit but I find it hard.

(Owner, 66)

My wife is seriously disabled, needing 24 hour care. We will not be moved from our home. No money or offer can compensate us for our home and way of life. It is unhumane that we should have this stress put upon us. We will not be removed, even with Compulsory purchase.

(Owners, 59 and 70)

It's a big worry to us what will happen. I get up in the morning worrying about it and I think about it all day. I've even started to dream about it. I dream that we've been chucked out onto the street with all our possessions and we've got nowhere to go. I've had two angina attacks during the past few weeks because of the worry. We don't want to move. We expected to see out the rest of our days here. We are not interested in the money. We just want to live in peace where we are.

(This couple, who moved into their prefab in December 1945, still have the original rent books which show their first rent was 15s 10d (about 80p). They were among the first couples ever to move into a Bristol prefab.

I am under my doctor for stress and I am taking pills to get a night's sleep worrying about your threat of Compulsory Purchase.
(Owner, 74)

Since I was told about what was going to happen [forced purchase and relocation] *I have had a stroke which has affected my quality of life.*
(Owner, 71)

Since the Prefab debacle started I have lost more than two stone in weight and cannot sleep.
(Tenant, 87)

Attempted suicide. Kill myself.
(Tenant, 66)

I have had more angina attacks since hearing we have to move. I think it's disgusting, disrupting people's lives.
(Tenant, 62)

Re above - I'm now being treated for high blood pressure, due to stress.
(Tenant, 67)

I am a multiple amputee.
(Tenant, 52)

Worries all the time suffering from strokes, that occur more often now because of stress.
(Tenant, 84)

Since this started, I regarded myself [as] *fit, but this year I am taking tablets for a health condition, also I have a stress problem which only hos-*

pital can sort out. Due to the way this City Council is going about all this heavy handed.

(Tenant, 81)

Now on anti-depressants. Loss of appetite and weight loss. No honest answers. In a state of utter confusion.

(Tenant, 44)

Yes, I have a heart problem and I am frightened all this worry will cause me to have a heart attack, having to wait two years to know what to do with my home. And if I last that long, where are you going to move me to?

(Tenant, 80)

Scared. Can't cope.

(Tenant, 46)

Because of the worry, I find that I am drinking more and more, mainly to help me sleep and take my mind off things.

(Tenant, 66)

A prefab is ideal accommodation for any disability and anything less than a prefab/bungalow is unacceptable. We have been informed there is no such property in the area.

I do appreciate all the hard work you are doing for prefab tenants / owners. Thank you.

(Tenant, 28)

Can't sleep - under doctor - all worry.

(Tenant, 81)

It's the stress that brings about sleepless nights, although I have capsules from the doctor. And I'm always getting more headaches.

(Tenant, 69)

*Yes, I am taking more tablets and seeing the doctor more often. Where are you going to move me to? No more promises, **please**.*

(Tenant, 70)

I don't think I could stand the stress of moving.
(Tenant, 83)

Since this has happened both my wife and I's health have worsened and I have spent the last three weeks in the BRI [Bristol Royal Infirmary] due to stress caused by being thrown out of our home, etc.
(Tenant, 81)

Seeing as I work nights I can not sleep during the days, which gives me very bad headaches and insomnia, which causes me problems at work and driving.
(Owner, 35)

FAMILY AND FRIENDS

My son doesn't understand the state I get in over this.
(Mrs. S.)

This is difficult evidence to provide. It could upset, revive guilt feelings, remind people of their helplessness.

Jacqui and David were active campaigners for their mother and mother-in-law, respectively. Dave in Bristol is currently aware of the health of his partner's 87-year-old mother.

The confusions and anxieties of residents caught in these schemes is shared with family and friends. As is the pleasure and relief of those ready and glad to move into new homes. Those who owned their homes had tricky decisions to make. To accept the valuations put on their homes, to sell to the Trust and buy again, or become tenants of the Trust. And, for some, to fret over what they would leave their families. Ken's calculations gave him five years of indecision.

One old lady dithered. For her own health's sake, her family pressed her to accept the Trust's allocation. She died shortly after. The inheritance, in this case, is a long remorse. Anxiety is infectious. Patience was often stretched: "It will be all right"...

"They'll take care of you"... "Don't worry."

The active generation, trying to support their elders, frequently had plenty on their own plates. Children, divorces, redundancy, illness... As problems go, moving to a new home could seem minor, not worth the 'fuss' it was creating. And elderly parents could be found straining to help their mature children. J. and his wife lost a son in an accident, days after their move. G's deepening confusion is for the lost boy, and also for the lost place and its routines.

One got glimpses. A 95-year-old woman stays all day in the kitchen of her new bungalow. Before, she'd get to the gate of her prefab, watch the world go by, chat now and then. She turns down the neighbour's offer to take her out. He tries to pop in every day. Her only visitor otherwise is a son (the other lives away, never appears) once or twice a week. He brings a supply of cheap ready-made meals. She doesn't like them, doesn't eat them, but is too afraid to say anything.

J. is as tough as they come. Over her mother's move, she is reduced to jitters. I wouldn't have believed possible in her.

"He never really got over it." "Never settled after that." "She'd been ill for some time." "Wasn't the same again." "It was too much for her." Sayings from the re-locations of the Sixties, I'm hearing again.

Pam makes no bones - her mother died because she lost her home in a slum clearance. But others are puzzled, bewildered, can seem 'half-soaked', simple. Can the Housing people really have ended their lives? What sort of world is it, if that is the case? Are people lost so carelessly? Not to be able to save your people, not to know they need saving, must be amongst the worst wounds of powerlessness.

A corruption in a democracy.

WHAT DOCTORS SAY

For older people in particular moving residence is amongst the highest risk factors for triggering an anxiety response and possible depression. It is only marginally less significant than death of a spouse.

Dr. Jeffreys, October 2001

Quoted by Professor Jolley in evidence to a court hearing relating to the closures of care homes for the elderly, February 2003. (Professor D. Jolley, BSc, MSc, FRCPsych, DPM (London), DPM (Manchester).

17 August, 2000

Dear Mr. Dumbleton

Thank you for your letter of 5ᵗʰ July...

> *I entirely endorse your observations. Regretfully there is a paucity of good research on enforced rehousing, particularly of elderly people...*

> *A house is first and foremost a home and it is this that is so often overlooked in any rehousing programme. Over the course of years there is a process of evolution in which the intense familiarity of every nook and cranny of one's home and a network of relationships and informal support develop which allows even the very frail elderly person to cope with every day living.*

> *In surveys (e.g.* Three Score and Ten *by Mark Abrams) asking older people what factors they regard as critical in providing quality to life, good health and companionship have always been reported as the two most vital ingredients.*

> *It has been my hospital practice for many years to arrange for older people who live alone or with a disabled spouse to have*

their final activities of daily living (ADL) assessment carried out by the hospital O.T. in their own home prior to hospital discharge. Many patients with a disability can cope with ADL in the familiar surroundings of their own home but fail lamentably when attempted in unfamiliar places. The social skills of people with memory impairment commonly lack flexibility to adapt to new surroundings. The great success of many voluntary "staying put" schemes has been to allow vulnerable old people to remain in a familiar environment.

A study which we undertook in Cardiff some years ago and later published in the Lancet showed that the mortality was lower in a questionnaire/nurse surveillance group than in controls in a large group general practice. Later the Welsh office funded us to carry out the same type of intervention in just over 10,000 people aged 75 and over living at home in South Glamorgan and Gwent. Although there was no specific research grant we did undertake a comparative study of the formal questionnaire/ nurse surveillance programme with an unstructured "over 75 screening" in 1,500 patients attending 3 group G.P. practices in Gwent. There were 66 deaths over 2 years in the formal programme as against 105 deaths in the informal screening group. The relevance of these two studies to the comments in your paper is that they may support your views that the enforced rehousing of vulnerable old people may lead to an increased mortality. To underline this point I refer you to a letter from a sceptical surgeon in the correspondence columns of the Lancet asking if we were claiming to reduce the mortality from cancer in our intervention group. Of course, we were making no such claim. What this surgeon illustrated was the belief, shared by most health service administrators, that old people can only die of catastrophic illness. As I have tried to teach for many years, a multiplicity of minor health deviations can combine to be of mortal significance.

It often requires a last straw situation to tip the balance.

I believe that the problem orientated questionnaire/nurse surveillance programme identified multiple small problems e.g. foot problems, impaired balance or gait, visual and hearing impairment, minor memory difficulties, depressive symptoms often unreported to the family doctors. These health deviations were usually additional to known disorders such as arthritis. It was attention to these more minor health impairments that reduced the mortality rate.

I am sorry to spend so much of my reply discussing some of my own work but I believe that it is pertinent to your assertion that enforced rehousing of vulnerable old people can be potentially fatal. Emotional trauma can be surprisingly malignant. Refusal of relatives to take back an old person following hospital admission is a striking example of emotional trauma leading to some old people turning their faces to the wall and rapidly dying.

I hope that these comments are of some value.

Professor John Pathy

President, Age Concern (Wales)

In December 2002 I sent the following questionnaire to seven GP s in Newport who covered the Prefab sites. A cardiac consultant who had expressed concern about patients also received one. The doctors were guaranteed anonymity. The issue was becoming politically controversial:

	Yes	**No**
Some of my patients are residents of the Prefabs and are involved in the rehousing scheme.	( )	( )

	Yes	**No**
I am aware that there is an increased level of stress amongst my patients who are residents of the Prefabs.	( )	( )

	Yes	**No**
If there is a noticeable increase in levels of stress, can it be said to worsen the health effects of the Residents?	( )	( )

Could you please indicate how you would rate any harmful effects on health?

A little effect   ( )
A moderate effect   ( )
A serious effect   ( )

Four completed replies were returned. All indicated increased levels of stress. Three that the stress would worsen health. Two indicated moderate effects on health. Two indicated 'serious effects'. (One of these was the cardiac specialist.) A student of handwriting might conclude that female doctors were more forthcoming in their comments.

Survey of Bristol Doctors

In August 2004 a questionnaire was sent to Bristol GP s who, we understood, covered the Prefab sites.[7] Since there are twelve sites in Bristol over 60 GPs were sent the survey. Many individual GP s might not have Prefab residents as their patients. And we probably didn't reach all the GPs who do have such patients.

This research took place just over a year after Prefab residents learned that they were to be cleared.

Sixteen replies were received - seventeen if we count the headof one GP practice, who returned all his/her colleagues' SAEs with the comment, "Unfortunately we are unable to complete your questionnaires (we receive far too many every week)."

---

[7] This circular was very similar to that sent out to Newport GPs

Doctors' Comments

i) Thank you for inviting me to take part in your survey. I have patients who are living in prefabs but not all of them are involved in re-housing schemes. I don't know what the consequences are of living in a prefab although I do imagine to be shifted round with little control and little say in what takes place, is likely to be very disturbing. However, I am quite sure that a survey of this kind cannot prove anything useful or robust when there are so many inter-connecting variables. I can immediately bring to mind one patient who lived in a prefab who is very happy to be there, provided he is not moved on, and one of our receptionists who moved voluntarily into a prefab and thinks it's wonderful.

ii) The only comments I have had are more pleased with their new homes or those who have refused them, preferring to keep their old ones - both happy -I have not directly questioned anyone.

iii) I've checked with all partners and although we are aware of the changes, the only patients we have seen have been relocated to 'new' accommodation already and are happy with it. Sorry can't help further

iv) I am not aware of any problems relating to prefab relocations amongst my patients. This may be because it has not been brought to my attention.

v) All people who go through uncertainty or moving house have some stress. This is the same problem as when nursing homes are closed down and people have to be moved.

vi) I'm aware of 2 patients very affected, both basically psychological stress rather than anything else, but clearly related to the uncertainty of impending moves, and not wanting to go. (The doctor ticks 'A moderate effect' in the box 'harmful effects on health'.)

vii) I have personally dealt with 2 affected residents. One is fine, the other has experienced anxiety and depression for the first time in her life.

viii) It is disruptive no doubt and some people worry more and go through an uncertain time. I have not seen heart problems or strokes as a result. (The doctor ticks 'A moderate effect' in the box 'harmful effects on health'.)

ix) The lady in question is finding the dispersal of her neighbours the most [hard to read word] thing and her depression has worsened in the context of social isolation. ('A moderate effect' on health.)

x) The doctor indicates increased stress amongst patients and some worsening of health as a result. "Though it may be transient." ("Depression on the individual" is described as 'a moderate effect'.)

xi) Enormously variable response for stress makes it impossible to be specific. Many patients are untroubled: some do seem to suffer worsening of symptoms - but this is true of whatever stress. ('A little effect' on health.)

xii) Quite variable - some accept the need to move without a problem. However, for others it is a source of significant stress and anxiety to see their house destroyed and be relocated, moving away from their friends, family and community can be a dreadful experience, causing both anxiety and depression.

xiii) Stress has a number of well documented detrimental health effects, which studies in the literature confirm, such as depression, anxiety, headaches, high blood pressure, stomach ulcers, irritable bowel syndrome, etc. It is also well known that moving house is one of life's biggest stressful events - and moving at an older age I am sure, is more stressful than for the average person. ('A serious effect' on health.)

xiv) I know one patient's dementia worsened significantly when she moved from Ashton Vale.

(This doctor has ticked 'little', 'moderate' and 'serious' effects on health with the comment: "in different individuals it has variable effect." She comments:

My patients who are residents in the Manor Farm prefabs, almost without exception, are made anxious by the prospect of moving. Many are long term residents, all are very happy with their accommodation and environment. My impression is that both their physical and emotional health benefits from the current environment (small manageable gardens and house keeps them active but not anxious), no neighbourhood trouble. I would say the Manor Farm prefabs provide a wonderful model of ideal elderly/disabled housing. It is reckless of the Council to destroy something so good.

R.A.G.E

The Relatives Action Group for the Elderly (RAGE), a campaign against the closures of care homes, and the relocation of their family members, are in no doubt that forced moves kill people. RAGE quotes figures for the extraordinary number of deaths occurring within weeks and months of such forced moves. Their cases have obvious relevance to the fate of the elderly and vulnerable in Demolition areas. The residents in care homes are likely to be frailer than the Prefab residents. They have probably lost their own homes and have had to make the tremendous adjustment to institutional life. Then that adjustment has itself to be adjusted.

The most obvious connection between the issue of demolitions and of care home closures is that both RAGE and ourselves both have to prove our cases to the powers that be. More than prove them. The fact that the elderly are made ill, are made more ill, and die destroyed by forced moves, occurs to their families as inescapable awfulness. The reasonable 'man in the street' with some experience of life and a little imagination, can grasp it.

But the powers that be won't have it.

RAGE has raised the funds to fight court battles against the closures. They are trying to use The Human Rights Act - specifically Article 2 (The Right to Life), Article 3 (the right not to be subjected to inhuman or degrading treatment), Article 8 (the right to a family and private life).

RAGE has not yet had a favourable court ruling. But a coroner in Lancashire is investigating deaths. RAGE hopes to make such deaths a matter of corporate manslaughter. The organisation has passed to us some of the medical evidence it has used in court hearings.

This is Professor Jolley, a Consultant Geriatrician, giving evidence in February 2003:

> *In common with Dr. Dalley, who has also produced a report on these matters for the Court, I have pointed out that directions from Central Government to reduce the capacity of the care home sector and improve the quality of environments within care homes, is producing a perverse impact which exposes current residents of homes and potential residents of homes, and other components of the elderly care sector, to considerable stress.*
>
> *I have reviewed what is known about the impact of relocation as an example of a stressful life event upon the mental and physical health of individuals and its impact upon their likely survival. Within this I reviewed the common sense understanding of the impact of such comments on the published literature drawing attention to its limitations and likely biases. In essence what is understood is that moves are stressful; they do produce physical and mental health morbidity and they can produce increased mortality. The latter is greatest in the first few weeks after a relocation and the impact is greatest on very old people who have shown previous vulnerability and who have concurrent pathologies, particularly multiple pathologies.*
>
> *Even raising the prospect of a move can, in itself, be seen to be*

stressful and when raised by others, can be seen as an intrusion on the private life of an individual. Such an intrusion followed by a requirement to move without the choice to continue a preferred lifestyle reflects a lack of respect for the individual who is required to move. It is possible to adopt strategies, which will minimise the impact of the relocation programme. These require tailored programmes of counselling and preparation for each individual and their families, and need to take into account their special vulnerabilities. These might include a vulnerability to anxiety and depression or mental infirmity associated with dementia. If individuals choose to remain within a group that will be relocated, there are specific considerations with regard to the timing of moves, the preparation of individuals and groups for the move, the preparation and provision of staffing and transport arrangements, and particularly the arrangements for continued and properly informed medical support. All these procedures are designed simply to ameliorate the impact of the stress of a relocation but they cannot take away that impact, and the impact will be greatest on the older people who have the greatest vulnerability.

RAGE point out the plentiful evidence from America and Canada, to be found via the internet. There has been a long-term funding crisis in the American care homes system, producing the same effects as we now see here in the UK. What we are looking at even has a name. Google yields some 2,000 references to 'Relocation Stress Syndrome'. (Some reports use the term 'Transfer Trauma'):

Research that has been done as early as 1970 on RELOCATION STRESS SYNDROME shows that the symptoms of depression, disorientation, serious illness and death, are more pronounced in the frail elderly. (British Columbia Health Coalition, December 2002.)

"As early as 1970"... Incidentally, recent research in the US is supported by the US government (via the US Administration on Ageing).

There are differences between demolishing what have been

permanent homes, and shutting care homes, and hence probably differing death rates. But the definition of Relocation Stress
Syndrome includes:

> Decreased ability to make decisions
> Loss of control
> Feelings of insecurity
> Anger towards people responsible
> Loss of social contacts
> Increased family conflicts...

Also changes are noted in sleeping, eating, orientation...

For the relevant medical knowledge we should not need to
cross the Atlantic, or turn on a computer. This is routine
knowledge on the local geriatric ward. But there is a British
Chinese Wall between Health and Housing. And between us
and our imagination. Regardless of what the doctors say, the
most visible distresses are not, somehow, to be believed.

STRESS AND HEALTH

At Daisy's funeral her son asked, "Do you think the stress [of
making her move] accelerated the cancer?"

Similar questions were asked at Newport. People were dying
of cancers. We knew some very severely upset by the upheaval.
Is there a connection?

Madeleine Bunting, in her startling book *Willing Slaves*,[8] documents the awful physical and psychological damage increasingly caused by overwork and workplace pressures.

She quotes one study: [In stress] "The process enhances one's
level of arousal because the cognitive, neurological, cardiovas-

---

[8] Madeleine Bunting, *Willing Slaves*. (Harper Collins 2004.) See especially
Chapter 7, "Keeping Body and Soul Together."

cular and muscular systems are stimulated as the body prepares for an emergency in response to a sudden shock. The heart rate is increased... Glucose stored in glycogen in the liver is released for energy, blood supplies are redirected from the skin to the brain and skeletal muscles and the secretion of sweat increases."

Stress, then, is characterised by "emotional vulnerability, persistent negative emotions, elevated hormonal base levels, hyperactivity of the automatic nervous system, so that the body never relaxes, and tendencies to experience psychosomatic symptoms. Over time this state of affairs may cause illness due to wear and tear on tissues." [9]

It seems reasonable to apply some of her findings to the plight of elderly persons in demolition schemes. Stress, whatever its occasion, has the same physiological effects, one may suppose.

"Exhaustive research," Bunting writes, provides a link between stress and "a whole range of medical conditions. Stress "triggers hormonal and chemical defence mechanisms, mobilising the nervous system for 'fight or flight' response."

Like many of her subjects, the old and ill at Newport, Bristol, or wherever in the demolition schemes, can neither fight nor flee.

Madeleine Bunting writes, "Stress can promote an already existing cancer or heart disease, or it can trigger these conditions in an existing vulnerability." (But she quotes no source or research for this statement.) This is a more cautious summary of researches, found on the internet:

'Is Cancer Caused by Stress?'

Researchers have conducted many studies to see if there is a

---

[9] Bunting is quoting from research by Sutherland and Cooper in *Employment and Health*. Ed. Jennie Grimshaw (British Library 1999). In *Willing Slaves*, ch. 7, "Keeping Body and Soul Together," p.195.

link between personality, stress and cancer. No scientific evidence has shown that someone's personality can increase their cancer risk. Although findings are conflicting, the feeling of being stressed does not appear to be a strong predictor of cancer. Major life stressors, such as divorce or the death of someone close, may raise cancer risk slightly. Also poverty is linked to higher cancer risk, although this may reflect health behaviours and poor access to medical care more than the stress of poverty. Of interest, several studies have shown that people who are socially isolated are more likely to die of all causes, including cancer. Whether this applies to people who have already been diagnosed with cancer is uncertain.

Perhaps age and disability are themselves 'socially isolating'. To be sure, the long anxiety about losing their homes was mentally isolating for some. If that does the same harm.

HEALTH AND INEQUALITY

Very thorough researches, using world-wide data, by Richard Wilkinson [10] prove that being powerless makes people live shorter and less healthy lives. The stress of disrespect, and low status, low esteem, does kill. The civil servants who stonewalled our efforts on behalf of the prefab people might like to note this research, if not ours: "A survey of Whitehall civil servants found junior ranks were three times more likely to die in a year than seniors."

JOINED-UP THINKING

Every letter, report, copy of interview or video we produced about the plight of the elderly in Newport's 'regeneration' schemes was sent to both the Housing and Health sections of the Welsh Assembly Government. Every reply was routed via the Housing Section.

---

[10] *The Impact of Inequality: How to Make Sick Societies Healthier.* (Routledge 2005.)

Once, after a special effort, a direct reply did come from the Health Ministry. It pointed out that Newport Social Services had responsibility for the care issues we were raising. There was no evidence on the ground that Social Services were making the extra effort required. (Indeed that Department was facing cuts through that period.) When we wrote to Social Services for details no reply came back.

The Welsh Assembly Government takes special pride in a Committee dedicated to the needs of the elderly. The first line in its 'mission statement' expresses its aim to preserve 'independent living'. That is, to do whatever can be done to keep people in their own homes for their health's sake. Medical officers of WAG have said nothing about the Prefab clearance, nor about the other demolition programmes in Wales.

Medical officers of Bristol City Council have said nothing about the impact on health and lives of the Prefab clearance there, either. Social Services spokespersons in both Newport and Bristol have also been silent about any impact on people's lives of these rehousing schemes.

The Director of Housing in Bristol was asked whether he consulted with Social Services before sending out his alarming letter to Prefab residents announcing demolition. The answer was "No." He knew Social Services had problems, were facing big cuts, he said. In the opinion of one tenant, Dave Drew, speaking in 2004, "It seems likely the thought never crossed his mind."

The Welsh Assembly Government, in almost every document it produces, repeats rhetoric from New Labour's reforming zeal. Joined-up thinking and policies, 'Corporate' approaches, multi-agency working, 'Holistic' solutions.

In May 2003 the Welsh Assembly Government did publish a document, *The Implementation of Social Housing Clearance Programmes and their Social Impacts* (HRR 4/03). This is a review of researches carried out into redevelopment schemes where and whenever such studies have been done. The point is to draw up 'best practice'. There is no original research, no up-to-date, or local content, at all.

There is no medical content. The advice is unexceptionable, emphasising the need to consult with the residents at all stages. No Local Authority or developer would say they do any different, these days. Consultation is the word..

There are very few bare statements here recommending sensitive treatment for 'vulnerable' residents. No cry from the elderly is recorded here. In essence, this is a licence from WAG to carry on demolishing without a qualm.

The consultants who wrote the review for WAG were HCAS Chapman Hendy - the same consultants who drew up the plan for the Newport prefabs, for the transfer, and it's financing.[11]

---

[11] See Appendix 4 for more details of the review, and Appendix 5 for 'Joined-up Thinking'.

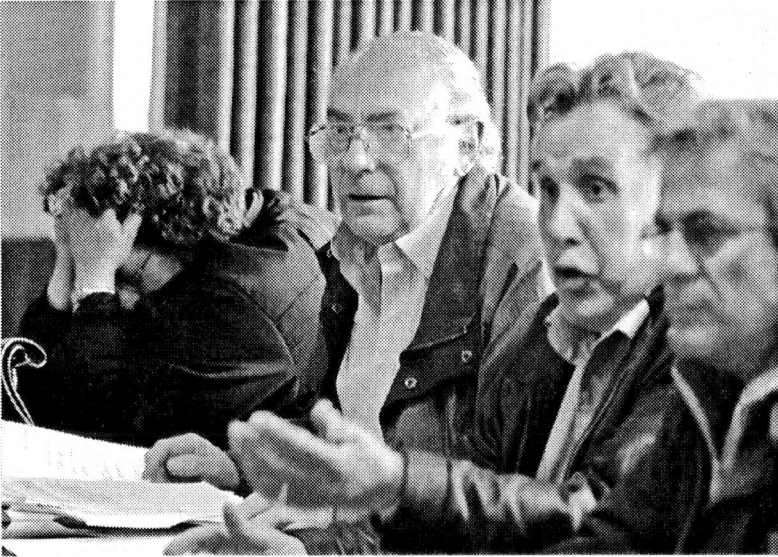

(Photo: Courtesy Bristol United Press)

The Council 'consults' with the residents. The 'Don't Know' plan, May 2006.

SECTION TWO

DOING THE DAMAGE

Our errors are caused by our good intentions as much as by our bad ones. That is very hard for us to grasp. It would really make us suffer not to trust our good intentions.

(Nietzsche)

I never knew in detail what the fear is.

(Jacqui Handley)

STRESS IS THE WORD

All that is going on affects them day by day and that effect grows the same way as cancer will grow in your body, so will this doubt and worry and strain grow in an elderly person. It's like cancer - it can destroy you.

(Pat Morris)

'Stress' is the word most used by the helpless residents. The word 'stress' comes from an old Greek word which means 'in a narrow place'. So 'stress' signified something like claustrophobia. No way out. Perhaps the Greeks had an ambush in mind. The enemy has your where it wants you.

Doctors tell us what we already know. Stress is inseparable from living. Stress can have many sorts of physical, mental, emotional and behavioural effects. It can lead to all sorts. Stress varies enormously, person to person. This one's challenge is that one's knock-out. From happily stretched to stretchered off.

People stated it simply enough. 'Stress' recurs constantly in what they said about their health.

It's the stress that brings about the sleepless nights, although I have capsules from the doctor - and I'm always getting more headaches.

(Tenant, 69)

I am now being treated for High Blood Pressure due to stress.

(Tenant, 67)

And from the same Bristol survey, the 'stress' came through as anger:

Let's have the truth - no more lies.

(Tenant, 81)

Tell the Council to be honest...

(Tenant, 83)

We have been badly let down by this useless City Council.
(Tenant, 77)

The Council have no feelings towards the old and disabled whatsoever.
(Tenant, 84)

We pensioners have been betrayed by a City Council which could not organise a raffle.
(Tenant, 76)

The Council should not be doing this to us at our age.
(Tenant, 87)

I have lost complete trust in the Council and wish that they could be more open and truthful with all of us for a change.
(Tenant, 57)

The Council are not of this Planet.
(Tenant, 58)

Council should be ashamed to treat us elderly in such an inhuman way with no regard to health factors
(Tenant, 68)

The Council needs to rethink their approach to the housing situation. Perhaps they should listen more to their tenants rather than to their experts.
(Tenant, 66)

I find it very unsavoury to inflict this on hard working innocent people through pure GREED.
(Owner, 67)

What the Council is doing to ageing and disabled people is disgusting. Where is our rent and tax going if they say they can no longer do repairs? It seems gain on their behalf is all they consider.

Anyone who owns or rents Council property could be **next**. *So* **watch** *and* **beware**. *For they will surely strike again.*
(Tenant, 71)

Perhaps 'fear', or even 'terror', are better words than 'stress' in this context. 'Worry', 'anxiety', 'dread', apply. And, as time goes by, 'apathy', 'withdrawal'.

'Stress' is over-used. It's a ready word for any moment of un-happiness or trouble. Typically for problems at work, or with 'relationships'. But perhaps life has become like that. Even more than the vast numbers of prescriptions for anxiety and depression tell us. The elderly forced to move 'are their situa-tions'. The present and future have been shrunk to this deep uncertainty.

In the narrow choiceless place.

Doctors respond predominantly to 'stress'. 'Fear', 'terror', don't have the same diagnostic value. 'Disgusted', 'sad', 'bro-ken-hearted', don't do the business. Sticking with 'stress' holds out the hope that a clinician will, one day, write 'Demolition' on a death certificate.

John wakes up "in a sweat and lather." He and his wife are living among their packed boxes. Errors mean their new bun-galow has not been fitted with the necessary adaptations. Glo-ria is semi-paralysed from a stroke. John hasn't worked for years because of an industrial accident. In recurring night-mares, the mistakes are all John's. He is a fool and a failure.

STRESS MAKING

Jacqui says it's the loss of control over one's life. It's the total disruption of routines, the massive shock to habits.

Pat says it's the number of years the whole process has to wear away the nerves.

Ken says it's the experience throughout that no one responsi-ble has any understanding of what it is like to be old and in-firm.

Mary seconds that: "They don't know 40, let alone 70." "No one is listening," she says. There's no one to call a halt to the distress as it happens. For Mabel it was "the papers, the papers." The tide of information coming through the door that she didn't understand. *"Everything* was a hassle," says Moira. (She's a witness that, for some, the induced depression doesn't go away with the new home - that stress stays put.)

The significance of these Newport witnesses is that, in many respects, the planners, the Council, the Trust, have done their best.

At Newport, the tenants voted for the redevelopment in very large numbers. (Owners were 'consulted'.) Five tenants were elected to the Board of the Trust. They sat alongside five Councillors and five 'independent' persons. Residents' groups were formed on each site and funded by the Trust to channel information back and forth - report difficulties, etc. A small team of Resident Liaison Officers was appointed to support people through the process. Residents were promised 'like for like' in the exchange of homes. And that 'no one would be out of pocket.' Residents had choices about the type of bungalow from five different models. And some choice of re-location and neighbour. Owners could choose to buy again, or become tenants. And the Trust can line up people to say this has all worked very well for them.

If the loss of control over your life is the central cause of stress, it may include the others: - the length of time these schemes take; the people who don't understand you are losing control; the information you can't take in; the uncertainty that descends on you. (Do you paper the parlour? Plant the garden this year?) You lose your grip on time. Lives were said to be 'on hold', 'in limbo'. 'Losing heart' said some.

The consultation and participation offered to Newport's prefab residents were designed to counteract just this sense of power-lessness. To be involved in the decision making process in-creases the sense of control. Active tenants' and residents' groups over the years have won their right to be consulted and to participate in housing and town planning matters that affect them. The Trust's structure of involvement with the Prefab residents could be said to be state-of-the-art.

But the practice belies the theory. Once in the maw of the Plan, those frightened by it all, those trying to oppose or change it, experience defeat.

It's in the daily doings. Mary in the 'glorified caravans' - the first decant homes used by the Trust - couldn't turn the shower tap on. "Oh, I can do it," says the Trust person, with a flick of her youthful wrist. The 80-year-old gent in the next caravan has to kneel to light the oven. He can't control that bit of his life.

Without the money to flee, you can't get outside the plan. Stating your case led you from pillar to post. The Council, Trust, Development Agents, contractors, all lined up with the Welsh Assembly. Councillors signed up to the policy, and even sat on the Trust. MP s wouldn't get involved on their local Party's patch. The transfer of the prefabs to the Trust from the Council's ownership denied the residents any appeal to the local government Ombudsman.

"I didn't go to the meeting [with the Trust] for the simple reason I couldn't stand to be in their atmosphere," says Mary. "They look over your shoulder when they are talking to you." ("They look through you," says Mr Berry.) "I knew I'd get so angry ... I don't want another turn in hospital like the last one" (Mrs Peggy Evans) "They don't care. I don't want sympathy; just that they'd do things they've promised and finish so you don't have to go on and on.

The Trust had a well advertised complaints procedure. It was complicated (four stages) and laborious. The Trust might headline how few complaints were received, or proved against it. Penny had the stamina, *nous* and support to pursue her complaint. It took over a year to extract an apology from the Trust

This is Jacqui Handley, as Chairperson of her Residents' Group:

> *Once you became part of any participation structure that is when things got really difficult if you wanted to participate, be involved and have real choices. As a group we were always realistic, we knew there wasn't unlimited money but we always felt they were far happier if we agreed that they were the ones with the skills, the information, the knowledge, all the other things that they were presenting us with, whatever it was, and we were only being there to say yes. And because we didn't always say yes it made our lives very difficult.*

> *We never did get to see the Business Plan. I did ask about the Business Plan. I actually wrote to the Council about that and also made them [the Council] aware we weren't happy with the Contract agreement they'd made with the Trust but nothing came from that...*

> *Going back to participation we did try to follow the routes they wanted us to. We went to the meetings and all that, but we never got anywhere and you got to feel you had to take it further and we'd write to the Welsh Assembly and what have you, really we're not being allowed to participate. All that I got back from the Chairperson of the Board was that each time we wrote to the Assembly we were holding things up because of all the work they had to do to reply to the Assembly. I was absolutely horrified when she said that.*

> *That's the whole idea - we were participating and could be made to feel bad about it. The problem is, as a group, we had some really skilled members on our Committee, they had had good jobs. They were there to think and work at things and draw things out of them. They could see different scenarios happening, it was very difficult. We did various reports. We tried to participate. We did reports on the effects on people, the cost, the health effects...*

The cure for stress adds more stress. It is bad faith to be invited to 'participate' when all the main aspects of the plan are already decided. Still, the residents' groups who supported the scheme, their representatives sitting in on meetings, the tenants elected to the Board itself, did probably survive better for their activity than the purely passive, or the angrily opposed. Taken together, the active pensioners for the scheme and those against, show what a democratic opportunity was lost. If they could have been let loose on the original plan, made it themselves.

The 'cure' by consultation at Bristol was farcical.

After the bombshell letter from the Council cancelling Plan A (the 'stay put' option), there were public meetings to explain the future. Billed as 'consultation' meetings. To packed audiences, five possible policies were outlined. Four were explained to be impossible. Clearance was inevitable. Owners resisting would be Compulsorily Purchased. Tenants resisting would be evicted.

There is some housing law that lays down what 'consultation' and 'participation' should be. It is weak law, but it is very likely Bristol Council broke it. We cannot afford to hold them accountable.

"If only they had consulted with us," says Mr Berry. He means if they had listened to him. For all the forms of consultation set up by the landlord, they didn't do that. He could have been saved the awfulness of the building site, [12] his paths would have been less dangerous, he wouldn't be in debt (for the first time) to the utility companies, he'd have been spared the charges for his disability adaptations...

"They made him very ill," says his sister.

Mr Berry is in a hard wrestle with his feelings. He likes his new bungalow very much: he appreciates his luck as to its position.

---

[12] See Appendix 8.

But he is badly jangled, eight months after moving in. "It's the way they treat you."

The Worst

My committee friends were made most unhappy by the falling out with neighbours. The people supporting the plan looked upon us as wreckers. To go about your business likely to bump into angry people, to pick up rumours of the harm you are said to be causing, is stressful at a fundamental level. 'Community' doesn't mean liking everybody, but it implies a degree of respect and toleration taken for granted.

We coped as a team, but un-neighbourliness penetrates personally. It caused us to behave badly. We walked out of the official talks in what must have seemed a spoilsport way. What wasn't seen was that constant hostility across the table had reached an intolerable level.

My friends could believe that the Trust was aggravating divisions amongst the residents groups; divide to rule us out. My line was that everyone had exposed nerves. Feelings were hair triggered, looking to blame.

Janet, Ken, thought me naive. Couldn't I see power politics under my nose?

The paranoia became equal. The Trust saw us, me, as politically motivated persons...

Self-assertion, power fights, adrenalin surges, may tell the young they are alive. Conflict can tell the old they are dying. The chemicals say fight or flee - and make symptoms when you can do neither. The plunge into weakness ('Your home is ours....') insinuates that all the life has been failure.

I'm going on the sick and scared expressions, the edging towards paranoia, and those who took up antidepressants for the first time since old traumas, such as bad divorces. And John's sweaty dreams of self-accusation.

There are plans within plans. People in what they are saying, are pointing to a tyranny behind the orders they have to obey. The privatising of council housing, the allocation of investment in public services, land values and the market, the landlord relation, are a swirl of forces. 'Consultation', 'participation', are taking the piss. My friends are belittled in a great weather front. And the bright young things spin nothing but sunshine.

HOME

> *'A joyous shot at how things ought to be'*
> (Philip Larkin)

Home is the world we have most control over. Or have to believe we have.

Is it necessary to prove that home is important to prove that some people die when their homes are demolished? Do you need 'research'? Isn't this something we might know about ourselves? A survey in France showed people rating home more important than work or leisure. Daft stuff. Our parts of life sink and swim together. What are we calling 'home', anyway? Building, family, place?

Children in orphanages know what home is. A homeless woman told me she felt "all the insecurity you can feel in this life". Exiles from their homelands spend lifetimes knowing what home is.

"Last Christmas was murder," says Mr. Trees. "Everyone going around with long faces, we'll be chucked out." Christmas is home in lights.

Everyone quoted in these pages is saying how important home is, whatever else they are saying. Nancy's "little grounding, my familiarity", is little enough, and huge enough, since her husband died.

Here is someone who has studied the subject:

The spaces within and through which we habitually live, tell you more precisely of where you belong. These things add to your understanding of who you are, of just how you figure in this society, in the wider scheme of things. It is thus that spatialities can literally place you. They can tell you where you fit in, let you know your relative power. [13]

Here is a man discovering his relative power:

Bob was torpedoed in the Atlantic war. In the lifeboat the men kept spirits up talking of the peace, and home. (Mr Trees telling this story to one of his neighbours is hesitating about being sentimental - telling an "old salt's tale".

Bob and his wife came to the prefab after the war. The news of demolition hit them amidships. She died. Neighbours believe 'stress' appears on the death certificate. Bob, under pressure to move, resists. He wants to stay with his memories. Neighbours are sure they will find him dead.

Such a story can seem sentimental. Because, I think we are used to looking up to power. Victims earn a sigh.

Home Owning

In Bristol, just over 100 Prefabs had been bought from the Council. Perhaps the owners had thought to increase their relative power. Home owning is supposed to earn more than its own reward in our housing system. At least these had reason to believe they owned the place.

*I truly thought we would be able to live **in peace** at Hadrian Close until the end of **our days** and feel safe and peaceful. It's just downright **rot-***

---

[13] D. Massey, 'Living In Wythenshawe', ch. 28 in *The Unknown City*. MIT Press 2001. And see Appendix 6.

ten that we have all the upheaval of moving from our homes we have bought, and you expect us to buy all over again. Paying the once is **enough.**

(Owner, 79)

For some reason the Council has overlooked the true value of owners' land before the prefab is taken into account! My land on prime building land is worth £200,000 plus with a government forecast of a 16% rise by December 2006. On top of that is the house renovations plus compensation.

(Owner, 56)

We bought our home and worked hard to improve it to suit us. We don't want to go back to paying rent for Council accommodation. We are happy here.

(Owner, 69)

How dare you try to take a home that has been in my family for 57 years.

(Owner, 50)

Replies and comments from the Bristol survey show very little difference between tenants and owners as to their feelings about their homes, their anger with the Council, their confusions... Perhaps a higher percentage of owners than tenants completed the forms and made comments.

With regard to health, 60 out of 82 homeowners state that their health is affected or an existing condition made worse by the threat of relocation. 18 out of 22 homeowners who indicated no health effects, mentioned they worry most days or all the time about what is happening to them. This is true of 51 tenants.

Janet is got very down by it all. "Because I'm on my own." Owning on your own, is different again.

Penny and Nancy used the relative power of owning to keep their rights, fighting off pressure and possible Compulsory Purchase. It cost. "They found my blood pressure was 190 over something"

(Penny).

The latest plan in Bristol saves half the owners if they choose to be built around.[14]

Attachments

I was out of my depth in Slum Clearance days. I don't know how Mrs. Murphy was in the Home. The Housing Manager refused to tell me where she was. "Confidentiality," he said with a smirk.

Then there were the three very old ladies in North Edward Street. ('Ladies' they seemed to me then, and now, 40 years later.) They lived together. All stick thin and frail. They moved around the house quietly, pooling their strengths. They asked me very earnestly to help them. They were very frightened. I muttered promises, but I never went back. It was all too late, if it had ever been early enough. The city centre site was worth millions. After years as a car park, luxury 'penthouses' rise over that spot. There was a Council promise to put back some 'social' housing. But that is as forgotten as the three ladies clinging to their niche, to each other.

Vivien Sholton, a student of photography, took stunning pictures of men and women in their Bristol Prefabs. The persons in the middle of their possessions are all of a piece with them. The proud and frightened faces say that. Daisy lifts her chin. Doreen clutches a dog. The old gent makes us smile with his jazzy jumper and the sofa which dwarfs him.

Vivien says she failed. She wanted to tell the story of the residents' distress. You have to know the story to be able to read these faces and bodies. The master painters did show-off pictures of rich people in their surroundings. These are show us mercy pictures.

---

[14] Plan C, the deal with Bovis, was announced with the promise that prefab owners would be saved by it. In the detailed plan half have to move. Another lurch and let-down. See Appendix 2 for Bristol's 'three plans' for the prefabs.

"It's awful," says Mrs. Pugsley, about her ageing, "I didn't think I'd have to start counting my steps." Routine, habits, attachments, are the ropes that get us over the last hills.

Penny was determined to stay put. The valuation put on her property undervalued what she and her husband had put into it. She feared her furniture wouldn't fit in the bungalow. She was preserving her life with her husband, and, in the fight with the Trust, her own tough character.

Home gives things life. Ellen, missing her things for the months she was decanted, said they had been her "personableness".

George is addicted to gardening. But the drainage in the new garden is bad. Stemming the last flood brought on an angina attack. The patio is not level, dangerous for the 91-year-old. The shed has been put in front of the kitchen window. He surveys his garden, that isn't his, with the weary knowledge that he hasn't the strength to get it right.

Stuff gets lost in the moves, the years (maybe) in store. Mary grieves over the last gifts her small children gave her. "It's not the money," Jenny insists, about their broken ornaments. She tells how she came by them. The removal man is rude: "It's your word against ours." Jenny is rubbished with her things.

Mary's cat went wild in the temporary caravan home, and had to be put down.

I was told about D., who died. She had been agitated a long time because her pets were buried in the garden, that would be reduced to rubble.

Can people die of such causes?

One elderly couple refused to move without their fruit tree. It caused a stir in the local paper. Readers probably thought them quaint, or even selfish. "What more do they want? They've got a brand new bungalow - people in Newport are queuing up for them."

Worry is hard work, on top of the physical effort. "I'm just so tired," says Janet in the months before and after her move. The Trust promised help at all stages of moving, but invariably people wanted to do their own sorting. What had to be to hand, what could be stored, etc.[15]

"It's always at the back of my mind." A woman with two years to go before the move takes over the front of her mind. To gain detachment from itself, the brain does apathy. The doctors do anti-depressants and sleepers.

"I feel more at home in others' houses than I do in my own." This is Pam, who has been in her new bungalow for two years. "I seem to go out to town less and I want to get back when I do so, but I don't want to be here. Daft, isn't it?"

Pam, like Mary, George, Jenny, go through busy motions of making their new homes home. Pam had been persuaded, much against her will, to move out of her prefab. The new bungalow represents injustice. She's been had - robbed. Moira, moved against her will, describes her strangeness as feeling "half-alive".

"It's not so bad when there are two of you. You can bat it back and forth," says widowed Pam.

Perhaps single people can be especially attached to places, pets, things, memories.

Jacqui's nightmares were of the people behind the doors they wouldn't open to her. What were they clinging to?

Pam describes how she has been detached from herself. Our attachment to people, places, things, attaches us to ourselves.

---

[15] See Appendix 7, 'Advice on Moving' (Newport Housing Trust)

Mr Berry considers his neighbours: "What I wonder is whether some of them that have passed on, god bless them, have done so because of all this stress .... I know four from round here in two years ... and Mrs S. went into a Home, she got very confused ... "By all this?" I ask. "Oh yes, definitely."

Mr Berry knew the old chap, a neighbour, who had killed his sister and then himself. I had attended the inquest and heard the most sad story, which had nothing to do with the prefab replacement. "Yes," said Mr Berry, "but perhaps deep down..." Pam and John had similar thoughts about that awful tragedy. I do not think it was connected. But our homes and our things, Pam, John, Mr Berry are discovering, are 'deep down'.

COMMUNITY IS THE WORD (1)

My friends and neighbours know where I am.
Will they still pass by me
I do hope they can
Oh! Please tell me soon
What is your plan
I'm thinking these things
I live on a corner, it's easy you see
They have to pass by and they share a thought for me
Will they forget me when they don't have to pass my door
I need the answer or I'll just worry more.
I'm a little confused

Mabel (93). A poem made from her words. She died shortly after the interview.

Mabel cried these words, and others, on a video film. A copy went to both Housing and Heath Ministers in the Welsh Assembly Government. Polite acknowledgements were all the reply.

Losing your neighbours doesn't kill you? Mabel dreaded the loss of passing people as much as she dreaded having to relearn her way in a new home. She was dependent upon others for practical help, for pleasure and, perhaps, for her sense of being alive.

'Community' is a word used by the residents for something they believe they have, and fear to lose. It is used by the 're-generators' for something they are aware of, and intend to re-create in their plans. It's used by the government. 'Sustainable communities' is the name of the latest game.

Voices from Bristol

Our home is one of the best places we have ever lived in. We love it here. It's not only the prefab itself, it's the community. I have been trying to tell people why the Prefab communities are so special. I have never lived with such nice, friendly neighbours. You have got to live here to appreciate what a nice place it is to live.
(Dave Drew)

I like very much where I am living. I have got very nice neighbours as you have got a job to find these days. I suffer from serious health problems and since I have lived at Ashton Vale my health problems are a lot better - and my doctor will verify.
(Owner, 56)

The community we have is lovely. Please don't change it. (Tenant, 54)

I am very concerned that if I am moved I will be a long way from my family and friends who I depend on.
(Tenant, 80)

This is a close knit community. We help each other. We don't want to be split up from neighbours.
(Tenant, 70)

I don't want to leave my home. I'm so worried about the process of moving.

I love the neighbourhood and my neighbours. Don't force me to move. I

love the peace and quiet - no problems, no noisy kids, no vandalism.
(Tenant, 66)

It is upsetting as I may have to leave good neighbours as we all help one another. I am bloody angry as I don't want to go anywhere else.
(Tenant, 63)

Very worrying - I want to stay where I am. I don't want to leave my next door neighbour and friend.
(Tenant, 86)

Am upset about where we will go - we love it here.
(Tenant, 72)

We had hoped to live the rest of our lives here.
(Tenant, 70)

There is nothing at all wrong with our prefabs, that a bit of woodwork and paint would not fix. Why can't the Council just leave us in peace in our wonderful community.
(Tenant, 56)

I want local, and don't want to move far away. My mother is disabled.
(Tenant, 50)

Would like to find another quiet spot like this, but I don't think there is much chance.
(Tenant, 70)

These are Newport residents in their new 'community':

I don't see anybody. I mean, I don't see anybody, not for hours, or for days, but I don't see anybody for weeks. (Ken Nicholas)

I won't say their names because I know they're worried about causing trouble. M. is very unhappy, very unhappy. He walks around, goes out. I see him walking around. He was by good neighbours, always talking to each other. Now he's shut in. J., if she had the money, she'd get out, go somewhere else. And I would.

(Mary Thomas, on her neighbours)

The elderly have been cocooned in prefabs for quite some time. Anybody who's been in prefabs over five years has become accustomed to it, the same way as if you're in a flat or a house for five years. The estate was an open estate before, we did see people every day, because there was only fencing up. Now we're being closed in. It's awful strange to them, the estates layout, it's all the newness they've got to get used to which you take for granted when you're young and find it quite easy to do. But you don't when you get older.

They're saying, Look, you've got a lovely new home, it's carpeted, it's cur-tained - but there's nobody of the right age bracket going in to help these people. These people have been getting up every morning and going to bed every evening in the same surroundings, and suddenly to take them out and put them in new surroundings, they do not get used to overnight. There's no follow up procedure suitable to certain needs of older people. Some of them don't talk to anyone.

(Pat Morris)

Gone is the dignity and respect
Gone is community spirit - none left -
Demolished, just like my home - flat.
Neighbours now interested if theirs is better than that
Not 'Good morning. How are you' or tipping of hats.
Heads are too busy looking around, and if they speak
at all now, it's if you've got more ground.

(Pam Sheen)[16]

The Newport plan kept residents (most of them) on their sites and near their old locations. The good intention was not enough, however. The years of demolishing and rehousing broke individuals and the ties that bind. In practice, land val-

---

[16] Residents trying to fathom their feelings could be 'hurt into poetry'. See Appendix 12. Mike Perrett, Ashton Vale, Bristol and poems from Newport.

ues, budgets, deadlines, housing crisis, car use... count for more than 'community'. The ordinary and everyday are fragile growths.

Architectural practicalities squeeze some new homes into corners, and stretch others out in unneighbourly rows. The best land on some sites is sold off to pay for the scheme. The bureaucratic 'Secure by Design' surrounds the bungalows with high fencing. For the sake of a safe 'community', people are cut off.

They haven't a clue about community - what it means, what it does for people.
(Dave Drew)

You have to see people, for a start. "Did you know the people living in the Prefabs?" Dave asked the Director of Housing about his notorious letter, announcing clearance. "We did when you told us," the Director replied.

For Dave, each prefab community is different. His Ashton Vale is a community, and Horfield and Brislington are communities. The officials and professionals who mouth, 'community' may think they know what they are talking about, but the reality is what passes between Dave and Daisy, Roy, Doreen...

Dave thinks it special for his Ashton Vale that the core of older people has gone through the phases of their lives together on that spot. It follows for Dave that each Prefab site should have its own plan. Local firms should rebuild as necessary. The subtle needs and sense of control are lost in the big deal, the giant contractor at work, the wholesale mentality. Community and communication are akin.

"There are no yobbos here," says a tenant about their peace. Ashton Vale is a blessed island in a more or less threatening sea of city noise. The yobbos are sending in the bulldozers.

(2) THE WORD 'COMMUNITY'

The word 'community' is more in use now than it once was. These are people I recorded in the 1960s and early 70s:

We lived here a long time. This is our home and we don't wish to move. I was born in this street. They are all neighbours round here. And we don't want to move from this area.

We are happy where we live, as we have lived here all our lives and are central to shops, schools, etc. If we have to move we will be put out of the way from all that we have been used to, and from our families and friends.

All my life in Byron Street round the corner. May have to push in with one of my sisters. We won't go anywhere else.

My wife and myself are elderly pensioners and we're both suffering from ill health and needing medical attention for the same. We have both lived in this house for 35 years and have reared a family. Housing kept in a good state of repair... .

I was born and bred in this area and my wife and I are well-known. It would be a great wrench to think of leaving here and the many friends we have.... This neighbourhood means a great deal to us.

Why I don't want to leave my house is because I am quite happy here. I have all of my relations around me, also friends. Shops are near, also town which I can walk to when I like and do not have to wait for buses. I have lived here for 35 years and in my old age now, I want to stay here. I go out to meetings and keep in touch with everyone. Once you are a long way out, we will be on our own, and I think the Council should do more and see that the houses are left where they are.

We have been resident at 29 Treharris Street for the past 46 years, having retired at 65.

I am now 75 and the wife 74. Having struggled to buy this house, and then saving enough to purchase the freehold on a very small wage, it was a great struggle for the wife to make ends meet, and so it is understandable that we feel so bitter about the very great upset , and the loss of all we have worked for through the years. We cannot hope to secure another house which will be so convenient to the shopping centre of Albany Road where we shop daily. We shall be moved away from all our friends we have known for many years. I go twice weekly to my institute to meet my old workmates and to miss this would be a great loss.

I worked on British Rail for 47 years, retiring as Yard Inspector, and it makes me mad to see all the heavy traffic cluttering up the roads which used to go by rail and did not worry anyone. We have close relatives buried in the cemetery and we very strongly object to the proposed road passing through the cemetery. We hope that all I have written will have some bearing on stopping this great upset to people just to give greater access to the motor car.

At our age - 80 and 77 respectively, and after 37 years living here and keeping our property as far as possible in first class condition, providing for our old age, it is heartbreaking to think of moving. I myself was born in this area and have been connected with St. Martin's church all my life, being secretary of the Mothers' Union for 13 years, but had to resign through very bad failing eyesight and arthritis of the spine. But all the members, young and old, are all very kind to me, not forgetting the clergy - the Vicar, Reverend Father Brown and Reverend Mr. Hayes. Also to my husband and I who are so well known in this area, we shall be losing everything and it is like the end of our lives. So we are praying, "Please God this road will never go through."

PS: We are greatly worried about what the Council will do with us, as we are elderly pensioners and owner / occupiers, but at our age cannot purchase other property.

I received your questionnaire, and should be glad to be of help in stating my case - i.e. if you consider I have anything useful (outside normal) to offer. My wife who is 74 and myself 78 - are both housebound, she as the result of a stroke four years ago, and myself - an operation for lung cancer in June 1963. Odd spells in bed until Dec. 1964 - an exceedingly grave pneumonia towards the end of 1965.

When I was ultimately discharged from Sully in 1968 Dr. Forman told me I was a very remarkable man - I repeat this in no spirit of bravado. But in September of this year I was rushed to hospital with a grave chest infection, and Dr. Thomas repeated Dr. Forman's statement. Since I have been on full strength antibiotics since 1965 you can understand how easy it is to become ill.

The Council refused a home help, despite the Council's instruction that it was essential to have one three days a week, minimum. This was when my wife returned from Hospital. We therefore have to pay our own domestic help, three days a week. She comes from Caerphilly. My daughter calls every day and does shopping and supervises things generally. She lives in Lisvane. Any rehousing will have to be such that both will be able to get to us without inconvenience. (Rent, of course, will be increased.)

A removal from here will, my doctor assures me, almost certainly result in our having to find a new doctor. After fourteen years with our present doctor and his unfailing care since 1963 (that means a weekly visit), this is going to cause us unimaginable mental worry and distress. (Incidentally, you may know my doctor as I understand he is Chairman of the Plasnewydd branch of the Association (Dr. Sh. Evans, Albany Road.)

People referred less to the general idea of 'community' or 'neighbourhood', 30 and 40 years ago, and more of their friends and neighbours, their own neighbourhoods. But, as with the Prefab owners now, it was financial uncertainty which kept them most awake.

Neighbours could include the dead:

My father and other relatives are buried at Cathays Cemetery in parts affected by this scheme, and I and my mother are very upset at the thought of the graves being disturbed.

I would like to point out also that this Road also ploughs through my father's, mother's, brother's and sister's [graves], also numerous relations' graves, if this order is passed.

Judging by the public meetings, anger about the dead exceeded that for the living.

(Angry Bristol voices now appear more despairing, even more violent, than these from 30 years ago. Perhaps people are less polite to power, nowadays?)

These people were threatened by a grandiose plan to put an urban motorway through some 1500 houses. Unfortunately for the planners these included solid middle-class homes. The ruthless campaigning targeted individual councillors, and eventually won the day. But the years of blight almost certainly did for some of the people quoted here. Life didn't win the vote to scrap the road, nor 'community', nor 'neighbourhood': property values won.

Every planned demolition now does Public Relations. Consultants consult - after a fashion. Contractors boast they are 'Considerate Contractors'. We are a bit better at geriatric medicine and awareness. Social workers do their best. Occupational therapists are called in. The 'community' sometimes votes.
Guess in which decade these comments were written:

Our house and neighbourhood mean everything to us, after having lived here for 63 years, and the thought of being made to move in view of old age seems heartless and cruel. I am 84 years of age, my sister 78, my brother 70 and my sister-in-law 67. My brother and myself are in extremely poor health...

I don't want to leave my home. I'm so worried about the process of moving. I love this neighbourhood and my neighbours. Don't force me to move.

Very worrying - I want to stay where I am. I don't want to leave my next door neighbour and friend.

*How is it possible for only eight people to create such HAVOC? Why are so many **unelected** people involved in making decisions? When has it been right for the Council to **Mislead** and outright tell **Lies** to both press and public? Will the Council now REMOVE THE TWO TICKS LOGO, "positive about disabled people" as the only positive thing they are doing is causing MORE SUFFERING!!*

I am very sorry about my writing, etc., I also have arthritis in fingers. Should you come to visit me it would be on a Sunday, as I attend Grange YMCA Welfare on weekdays. I was born 26.12.01. I was at sea and my ship torpedoed in October 1914. I was two months less than 14 years of age. I have travelled this world twice. No education, but vast experience... Our Queen must find it hard to provide OATS for her racehorses. No wonder Capitalists breed Communists. I sometimes wonder why this country does not (I can't pay for gas.) **Revolt.**

(3) FAMILY AND KINSHIP

The first and most famous study by University people of up-rooted 'community' appeared in the mid-1950s: *Family and Kinship in East London,* by M. Young and P.Willmott. The authors followed families in a move from Bethnal Green out to an estate in Essex. They measured as they could the family connections, the number of family visits made before and after the move, what people said about their neighbours, and so on. The point of the survey was to see whether the move was a happy or unhappy one. The answer was mixed and inconclusive (more time would tell). But the authors ended with the mild recommendation that home and area improvement might serve people better than wholesale demolitions.

Some 20 years later, this came to be policy in many towns. The money had run out for new 'green field' sites. And the demands of the town centre developers had been met for the time being.

Another influence on such studies of 'community' was that of architecture and town planning. We owe the close-packed, 'close-knit' estates of the 1960s to the attempt to re-create 'warm' community spirit. Examples quoted here - Glyntaff, Chapel Hillside and the Billy Banks, Penarth - are from the disastrous side of these experiments.

They were working in effect, we might say. The notion of 'community' was taking some hold. Tower blocks may even have been thought to do the trick.

Towns and cities changed, and the media picked up from the sociologists the headline 'Death of Community'. No one seems to have noticed the real dying of the elderly and ill. Willmott and Young have only one sentence about the upheavals for the old. About a resident of 60 years: "She had been shocked to hear that the authorities might be labelling her beloved court a 'slum', and was terrified lest they pull it down."

For all the terrified elderly persons in the 1950s, that is the only 'official' reference I know.

Sociology made its name studying the great changes to post-war cities and lifestyles (in the United States too). Sociologists counted all sorts, but not, it seems, deaths by demolition. Ways of life, but not this way of death. Perhaps without the proof of death certificates, it couldn't be done.

Willmott and Young write of 'kindly administrators'. Academics had to have access to records to do this work. Politeness is necessary. The gent who has produced the best book on prefabs and their history contradicts my nasty remarks about Newport Housing Trust. [17]

I did, in the late 60s, write in an article for a Town Planning magazine, declaring that people died of Cardiff's redevelopments. (I was thinking of Mrs Murphy, and the old man in Canton with the bad heart who was crying as he thumped the walls to show how solid they were.)

This comment was edited out. I don't remember making a fuss. I was too pleased, I expect, to see my name in print.

(4) WHICH COMMUNITY?

---

[17] Greg Stevenson. *Palaces for People* (Blatchford). In personal correspondence Greg wrote: "In my experience Newport Housing Trust has taken great care in their rehousing to make everything as stress-free as possible." The Residents Committee looked frightened when I read that out to them. Then Penny said, "Bullshit."

The community sends in the bulldozers to destroy these communities. The community needs the land, higher building densities, new roads... The national community, represented by Government, needs these policies, these levels of investment and private 'partners'.

The meanings of 'community' trip over each other. There's neighbourhood -'everybody knows everybody' - the help in time of trouble, a myriad daily deeds, the 'unpublished virtues of the earth, the 'little nameless unremembered acts of kindness and of love'.

And there's the 'business community', 'farming community', 'European community'. The combination of people, peoples, around, basically, an economic and political interest.

The community of Mabels, Murphys, Daisys, Jacks, Daves, Moiras is lost in translation to 'community' without an anchor - without recognition as a life force - a recognition that would allow the Mabels and Murphys the right to stay put.

The campaign by prefab residents in Bristol against clearance, with demonstrations at Bristol's Council House, was the community in action. The Tenants and Residents Association at Glyntaff (note the togetherness of tenants and homeowners in this case) decided much of their own future. In action, 'community' takes on meaning. Passive 'community' is a sigh for what's going, going, gone. Nostalgia for the future.

(5) SPIRIT

People are popping off all round. Mind you, they used to call it Boot Hill before, but at least you could see people walking around. (Nancy, on the new estate)

The areas under threat, under promise, of regeneration, are poor places, nearly always. They can be known for their 'community spirit'. That might refer to the defensive living that has to be done, co-operating to survive. From the outside we like to believe such 'spirit' is compensation: people who can't afford a good time can make up for it in other ways.

The 'c' word is slippery, but its use can cover real conflicts of interest. Campaigning against the clearances of homes and the property developers in the 1960s and 70s, I discovered that my own Pension Fund was invested in the deals. I'm drawing the dividends now.

The largest investor at the time was the Pension Fund of the National Union of Mineworkers - just as the Valley communities up the road were falling sick of male unemployment.

The word 'community' suggests that we meet, know each other face to face. But the face-to-face meetings elsewhere decide whether communities, and the people in them, live this way or that, or not at all.

Of course, people were often lonely before the Plan and the bulldozers, and before the policemen and architects hit on 'Security by Design'. The visits of relatives and carers couldn't fill all the empty hours. (Time weighs the same for the widows in my middle-class road. Loneliness isn't a class-based suffering.)

Bill's visit to his 95-year-old neighbour is all the human contact she has most days. Jack does a round of check-ups. People keep you talking. Tell you their lives.

Kindnesses to the Mabels may be their all in all. But what we are protesting to protect is a thin atmosphere. The Community Centre promised in the scheme has been postponed and relocated to the edge of the estate. Someone with the community at heart might have built this first, to help people through the turmoil.

Council housing was created when the British were feeling communal because of the World War. (Maybe also feeling scared of revolutions.) The Prefabs came out of a similar class truce in the Second World War. The scale and quality of public sector housing have, more or less since, been decided by the back and forth of economic interests gaining and losing political power. The cares and costs of creating decent living spaces created a 'post code lottery' long before the Post Office invented post codes.

The most pleasing estates in Cardiff, where I write, were 'socially engineered'. As were the 'failed communities'. A process blithely lied about. Tenants were selected for the good and the not-so-good areas, according to their jobs, appearances, etc. With decades of knock-on effects to follow...

'Keeping the community together' was the second big slogan of the Newport prefab replacement plan. (The first was 'new bungalows for all'.) And that idea hlped change Bristol Council's mind about scattering prefab tenants across the city. So there is some power to its elbow.

These years in Newport could demonstrate how much power in practice. How much power compared to budget power and profits in the construction industry. How much compared to the architects' brief. And how quickly the good intentions can evaporate when the customers turn awkward and resentful and promises can't be kept. Language is manipulated and scape-goating and divisive tactics become reflexes. Solidarity under stress, in these top down plans, just breaks.

There are signs in Bristol of how hopeless is the case. There will be very little left of the community that existed in 2003 by the time new houses arise in the next five, six, seven years. In Ashton Vale now, a vacant bungalow has been allocated to one of the Prefab owners. Disappointed tenants are furious. When 'communal' relations turn bad ways, they do so with especial sourness.

(6) KNOWABLE COMMUNITIES

They know the secrets. (Ashley)

We could keep old people alive better if we didn't have to appeal to pity or charity or obligation. If we knew their losses are our losses. Listening to the old men who went to sea as boys, the Newport, Bristol, Cardiff sailors of the wartime Atlantic, I learnt more history, more of myself. Daisy and her husband survived the siege of Malta. (Daisy cycled over 20 miles in the 1930s to begin her 70-year love affair with Bristol Rovers.) Nancy worked through Newport's industrial prosperity and decline, dodging sexual harassment the while. Denied a working life by an early accident in the steelworks, John's humour keeps our spirits up. J, put into care as a child, fosters all the children she can cope with. In a brief interval when Peggy (80) isn't agitated about her unwanted move she talks wonderfully about her time and travels ... Then the trap closes again.

Demolishing places and people cuts off all the stories that ground what community we have in real dimensions. The people I got to know had braved and were braving all sorts. I was learning how unordinary everybody is.

And the militancy and friendship of Janet, Jacqui, John, Penny, Nancy, Ken, Peggy, Bill, Moira, Pam, Dave, Jane, Lyndon... invigorated a stale activist.

From school and work so many experiences divide us. With ageing, more life is lived in common: failing bodies, increased dependency, surviving losses, borrowing courage, immediate pleasures...

The old can be good at solidarity. They live in the present. Which is something we might acquire from them. Free from the power of the past and the ambitions of the future. In groups together there is a lightness of being, a mild equality as a strong consolation.

Since William, a Newport tenant, lost his wife, his daily objective is to get out of the bungalow and find people to talk to. This urgent need of his offers perhaps the simplest and most intense definition of 'community'.

SECTION THREE

ONE THING ON TOP OF ANOTHER

All comfort in life is based upon a regular occurrence of external phenomena

(Goethe)

SURVIVAL COURSE

The point has, perhaps, been sufficiently made. But for the 'professionals' it might be useful to describe more of the when and how the process pinches, and the accumulating ordeals that the demolished have to weather, if they can.

DECANTING

The two moves required of many in the re-housing process is a major cause of stress.

A number of prefab residents in Newport had to spend months (some more than a year) in a temporary home while their new homes were built. This is 'decanting'. The Bristol residents, in their present limbo (autumn 2005) are hoping to avoid this. They have had sort of promises that one move only will be required.

I know the people who've been moved into mobile homes have found them dreadful, totally unsuitable - the coldness.
All right, they're nice and new, but they're not suitable for the elderly. They may be suitable for two weeks holiday, but for [the] eight or nine months some of these people here been in there - it is totally wrong. If you are twenty, thirty, forty or even fifty you can get over these things quite easily. Your mind can adjust to them. But it seems that once you have gone over that sixty or sixty five lines, your mind doesn't adjust. It starts to drop lower each year. A small thing becomes a big thing.
(Pat Morris)

Efforts were made at Newport to assess who could and who couldn't stand two moves. But it did not entirely work. Mary (71) suffered in the "glorified caravan" that was used in the first phase of the scheme. "We were the guinea pigs," later the Trust moved in superior mobile homes and used empty pre-fabs, and some of the new bungalows.

I related the torments of George (91) and Jenny (71) in their two temporary homes, earlier.

The easy chair next to the bed is 'chief nourisher' for so many plagued by insomnia. George is clinging to the sides of his favourite armchair as he describes the discomfort of the months without it. Mr. H. winces as he recalls his months on the 'banquettes' in the caravan.

"The main trouble was, we were told 12 weeks, and it turned out to be 38." Ellen was at Glyntaff in an empty house. They were able to take their three-piece suites. For Ellen, "It was worth it." After the decanting, the refurbished home was a treat. But she describes the temporary living as being "naked". They couldn't put up pictures, put their personal stamp on the allocated place.

Ellen watched Margaret and Jack, one of the few older couples on the estate, go down. Margaret sat staring out of the window. She wept most days. Her main loves were talking to neighbours, and gardening. (Her giveaways still bloom in my pots.) Her misery "can't have helped Jack." And walking up the hill every day to see the progress on their home may have contributed to the fatal heart attack.

Margaret died recently. Unpacked boxes were discovered - several years after the decanting.

This is the best detailed account I know, written by Melony, a young adult:

When I heard that the house I was living in with my parents was to be refurbished I couldn't have been happier. Our house, I felt, was desperately in need of refurbishment. Lack of investment by its landlord through the years had taken its toll, and the cracks were literally starting to appear.

We were told that while our house was being refurbished we would need to move into temporary accommodation. This would be a three-bedroomed house in a street close by. As the date of our move came closer we started to pack up our belongings. Although we knew we needn't physically move any of our belongings, packing up an entire house and a lifetime of memories was not only a physically draining but a very emotional time - and we were the lucky ones who were fit and able - not all our neighbours were. Lots of our familiar but non-essential belongings had to go into storage, as although our temporary accommodation had the same number of rooms, it was a lot smaller and did not have the same storage space as our own house.

Moving into our new accommodation was both tiring and disheartening. You see, we hadn't just left our home; we'd left our neighbours. I'd grown up with these people on my doorstep, and now they were scattered all around the estate. This left me feeling vulnerable, almost as if some network of support had been stripped away from me. I know that I wasn't the only one to feel this way. Almost everyone I spoke to commented on this aspect of our move.

The fact that we were now living in a smaller house raised problems we could not have foreseen. Our actual living accommodation was smaller, which made us feel almost at times claustrophobic. I felt that someone was always in my way - we were always having to squeeze past each other. We seemed to be arguing a lot more over trivial things that would never have bothered us in our own house. This caused me and my younger brother to spend a lot more time in our bedrooms. The family began to interact with each other less and less. At times I felt if we'd lived there much longer, we could quite easily become strangers.

The rooms in the decant house were all painted magnolia. They had no individuality. We were told that we were not allowed to hang pictures or mirrors, which upset some of our daily routines. The only mirror to be had in the house was one that had been perched on a window sill in the bathroom. All this just added to the feeling that we were living in someone else's house. At times it felt like we no longer had a home. It made relaxing difficult. I remember waking up one morning thinking what I would give to be able to knock some nails into the walls and put up some of my pictures - just to pretend that this house was home.

I started to suffer with depression, and it wasn't long before I had to give up work. Talking to my old neighbours made me miss my home even more, and I knew many felt the same way. As time dragged on several of my neighbours became desperately ill and, although the move was not responsible for their illness, to my mind it wasn't doing their health any good to be in unfamiliar surroundings, feeling isolated at times as many of us felt.

They had initially told us that we would be moving back in October, but as the date grew nearer we knew there was no way that the work would be completed on our house. Then we were told it would be November, but November came and went and we clung to the hope that we'd be back home for Christmas. I remember feeling disheartened each time we'd be given an approximate date, only to be let down. We took our Christmas tree out of storage and resigned ourselves to the fact that we'd not be home for Christmas. We tried to stay positive, and if I'd see a neighbour from our old house, the conversation would always be, "Well, it won't be much longer now and we'll all be going home."

As much as we all wanted to be back in our old homes none of us looked forward to the daunting prospect of having to pack up all our belongings for a second time. The weeks after Christmas dragged, and eventually we were given our moving date.

We moved back to magnolia-coloured walls, but they were our walls. Within hours pictures and mirrors were hung, and our house felt like home again. Day by day our neighbours moved back in around us and at last we started to feel as if our lives were ours again, not overshadowed with thoughts of packing and moving dates.

However, as I said earlier, several of our neighbours had become desperately ill, and within a year we had to attend three funerals of friends living in our neighbourhood - for with all the stress of the move, they barely had time to enjoy their refurbished homes. And even now, years on, this is occasionally commented on. It seems so ironic.

Our house is a picture now - new kitchen, new bathroom, no outstanding repairs, warm and cosy, quite the opposite of what it was. But it's left us all with the anxiety of what if they missed something during the rehab? We couldn't face another forced move.

Melony and Ellen's (and Margaret's and Jack's) decanting was organised by a landlord very anxious to please. The Glyntaff estate has a concentration of vulnerable people. It is a typically poor estate. Most demolition or rehabilitation schemes are likely to take place in just such places. Glyntaff is rated as one of the areas in the United Kingdom with the highest incidents of chronic ill health.

Moving day can itself be fearful. Prefab residents report exhaustion and emotional turmoil. Ellen and Melony describe more 'nakedness' - the inside outside, what they had exposed to view. (Melony hides what she can with duvet covers.)

Moira and Peggy both collapsed on or near moving day.

Ellen became anxious over the shabby carpet, and a stained stove, in the much-used temporary home. The next occupants would think her dirty, she said. She had the carpet industrially cleaned, and worked half the night before leaving. Home is trial and judgement, as well as home.

LIVING ON A BUILDING SITE

Researchers have taken photographs of cochlear hair cells irrevocably damaged after only one exposure to a very loud noise.
> (Diane Ackerman, *A Natural History of the Senses*)

The work takes years of heavy lorries, JCBs smashing prefabs ... and mud.

Jacqui kept guard as she could:

[It was] *the way the sites were left ... It was unsafe, stressful, dangerous.* {Jacqui gives examples: mud, pools of water in pathways, insecurely boarded over - no lighting, and the work going on "right up to the kitchen window."] *That sort of thing is unacceptable.*

Then they saw me with my video camera. It was the way I worked ... If you said something, they'd say it wasn't true. It was the only way I could get things to work for me. As I was filming, lo and behold the men started to erect the fencing [that should have been there in the first place].

They'd been laying pipes at the Stelvio estate... There were five inch pipes sticking up out of the ground ... silly things that shouldn't be. But it was a health and safety issue, could cause an accident, and you'd have to get on to it so we didn't feel responsible ourselves.

Penny (in her seventies) ran a regular obstacle course. Coming home, she found the path dug up. Planks were fetched for her to totter over. Penny came to feel she was being 'got at' because she was at odds with the Trust about moving. How did they do that?

By shutting me off from the world outside with corrugated sheeting and there was no need because there was nothing in front of me. They said it was for my own safety but that was stupid, because I felt more vulnerable with the sheeting.

I wouldn't know if there was anyone in my garden when I came home at night. Nobody could see me from the road. The postman and delivery people couldn't find me. It was as if I didn't exist.

At other times Penny's water, gas, electricity, telephone, were cut off. Her garden fence was damaged - grass and weeds allowed to invade. When the corrugated sheeting came down, the contractors piled materials a few yards from her door, even though compounds had been designed for that.

Penny never had any warnings, any advice, any apologies.

The Prefab Residents Association at Newport asked for a Major Works Agreement. A negotiated document would give the residents some say in working hours (start and finish times, weekend working...) and conditions, including information, liaison, clearing up... It did not happen.

The Association at Glyntaff did secure such an Agreement. The main contractor was replaced halfway through the scheme, partly because of the residents' complaints.

Peggy and her husband wince as a lorry rumbles past. "All day long"they say. It doesn't sound too bad, but they are older and they've had four years of it. "I've only been out on my scooter once since we've been here," says Mr. Evans, referring to the muddy roads and pavements. [18]

Pat Morris believes it's the overall length of time that kills people. Jacqui argues that it was a fault to work all the five sites at the same time. More time, more care? More time, more worry?

Bristol's first plan for their prefabs took its time. It allowed people the choice to stay put. The piecemeal replacement of prefabs minimised disturbance to the people moving, and to the neighbourhood. Penny's hips and Peggy's nerves would have survived there.

The blocks of flats at Penarth have been emptied. The demolishers and re-builders will not be working around people. But the six years of gradual moving out had its own miseries. There's the creeping blight of steel shutters, broken lighting, overgrowth, roaming children and youths.. dispiriting in themselves, and a telling pressure on the anxious decisions about what offers of re-housing (when and where) to take up.

The building site, the running down estate, provide a natural amenity for certain youths. Some fearful statements by the residents may belong to the general 'moral panic' about young people. But one woman did die of a heart attack, immediately after confronting a defiant gang. Her husband did not report the incident, didn't 'take it further'. Jack, the good neighbour, is telling me about this. We don't understand the man letting it go, or we understand too well. Another one down to 'natural causes'.

---

[18] See Appendix 8.

"Everybody in the street is out to do me." A builder speaking. Not a Lovells or a Bovis, but a man responsible for an Area Improvement Scheme - 100 or so houses. Complaints, 'extra' demands, threaten his margin of profit. It's the logic of a battle.

'The Considerate Contractor' is advertised on all the building sites in Newport.

Awards are awarded.

Officials from Lovell's can get good reports from residents. But the impact of the building works on this elderly population has to be great. The deadline and the sub-contractors are daily pressure. With some vulnerable 'customers', levels of 'consideration' are required beyond any on offer. And, apart from Jacqui's camera, no power is telling them.

FROM A VIEW...

No one died from losing their view. As far as I know. It is part of what is defeating Moira; she laments the green view she once had 'front and back'. She, like Mary, is taking anti-depressants again.

Mary is sad and angry in turn. She first lost a 'wonderful' view when she movedfrom a home on a hill to the prefab because of her mobility problems. In the bungalow she sees no one passing, only her own impossible-to-walk-on garden, fences and roofs.

Three Prefab sites at Newport are on hills. Many residents had tremendous views over the Docks, the Bristol Channel and the Avon and Somerset coastline. Even at Treberth, the largest site, many could look out on green hillsides with mature trees. Virtually all prefab windows gave access to some expanse of neighbourhood gardens, walkways, and people on their familiar errands.

The new bungalow dwellers look out on security fences on

most sides. Some fences are raised higher on retaining walls, or sloped gardens. Over the fences, the roofs of other bungalows meet the eye. Front door views are often onto the street, and the uniform bungalows opposite. Many front gardens are tiny or non-existent. At Stelvio, new houses and garage blocks look down closely on top of bungalows. This is on former Prefab land, sold to pay for the re-development. The distance from new house windows to new bungalow windows is on, or below, the permitted Building Regulation (Guideline) limit.

Carol is close to her claustrophobic limit in one of these bungalows. Jenny, in another, says she's not claustrophobic, but is bitter about the walled-in view from her bedroom. She spends much time there with a chronic condition.

Pat has lost, to my eyes, one of the best views in Newport, from high on the Ridgeway. He never speaks of this, although he is subtle and eloquent on everything that has happened to his neighbours and himself. I wonder if he doesn't care, or cares too much. His own philosophy is to 'get on with' things.

I'm afraid to ask him about the view.

Pat has a steeply raked garden. His bungalow is a few metres down from where his prefab stood. His bit of the hill is now enclosed behind the fencing. For the 12 months while the gardens 'bed in', the Trust pay a firm to cut the grass. Pat's own first effort had him falling into the machine, badly cutting his toes, and in hospital for nearly two weeks.

I only heard one person say directly that she liked the privacy in the bungalows. Only a few commented on the lost views of landscape. Very many commented on the lost views of neighbours passing.

John Ruskin, travelling by train through Wales 150 years ago, noticed that his fellow passengers "never once" looked out of the window at the "most magnificent scenery in the British Isles." In the harsh life, the internal scenery dominates the view.

The views from the Billy Banks flats and maisonettes in Penarth were also tremendous: over Cardiff Bay, the Docks, Cardiff City, and the hills beyond; and to the opening to the Taff and Rhondda valleys. A view to add to the value of the private homes that will replace this Council estate.

The people scattered from these homes had their minds concentrated on the when and where to go to. If they waited, would they come off worse... What pleased the eye and consoled the spirit in the ever-changing landscape, could not be afforded...

Shirley liked her views at Penarth. They were, I think, secret recompense for the heavy stigma on the estate.

Few ever speak about the lost views. What they miss, according to Shirley, is "that part of town". The old neighbourhood is missed for a surprising number of years. Pam sounds like an amputee who doesn't know what's gone. Dead husband, grown children, her home. The water birds she could watch on the pond. The past has been cut in two, and people are sadder for it.

Rich people pay for large views. Seeing far and looking over are integral to the larger life they can command. Our holiday views are theirs for keeps.

Unequal views of the sky mean unequal light. I heard complaints about the dark in bungalows at Stelvio, Ridgeway, Gaer. Kitchens that need lights on early and often. Living rooms half dark. People blamed themselves for choosing the wrong model bungalow.

When Mary, Moira, Carol, Chris, Jenny, Pam spoke about their lost views, I would try to weigh the feelings behind the words. How depressing, regretting, resenting... But, like trying to weigh, 'I love my home,' 'I love it here,' 'I love this place,' to know the weight, you would have to know the lives.

No one campaigned for their horizon. Architects did what they did - 'just like that,' Costs and land values dictated to the architects. And, as Jacqui explains, people are brought up to be grateful for what they get.

They next generation is already queuing up for the bungalows. They won't know what they are missing, or who went missing.

Mrs. S. sounds dotty. She's doing a radio interview - what her prefab means to her. She's on about the birds and hedgehogs. This is Bristol's £100 million re-development rolling up her road. New bungalows promised for all. Mrs. S. is cracking up.

There is research, apparently - which indicates that hospital patients with a view from their bed, their ward, are likely to do better than those without a view. (Who would have thought it?)

Mr Berry's shed was placed with its windows a metre away from a brick wall. Turned around, the view was a great stretch of the Bristol Channel and the Somerset hills beyond. Would the workmen have sited their own sheds so?

"ATTENDANT WORRIES" (Mrs Pugsley)

In a weary voice the old chap explains they have had four addresses in a year. Prefab, mobile home, plot number of the new bungalow, final address. He asks me to imagine the phone calls and letters they've had to make to all the offices and friends notifying each change. Post has gone astray. His wife missed a long-awaited hospital appointment.

"They offered us £60 for the garden. I wouldn't collect the money." He showed me photos of the vivid borders and the clever woodwork they'd spent 21 years creating. (This same man told me of how he had enlisted underage in the Merchant

Navy. At 15, he had been on the Atlantic run. The bombers and submarines were one thing. "I was too young, I suppose, to take it in." The real awfulness was his incurable sea-sickness. He laughs, is not boastful.)

The bungalows all have the same power supply company. To revert to your own, original supplier, you had to close this account and restart within 28 days. Confusion, missing bills. (Janet is told she needs to quote her post code to switch back. She hasn't got one. The Post Code man tells her it is taking 18 months to post-code the new estate.) A year after moving Janet is still not clear on the utility bills. Each week more phone calls, more hassles.

How many phone calls did you have to make about that problem?" I would ask. People pulled faces, shook their heads - it was too wearying to count or recall. Pat did count. It took him 11 calls to three departments to get his 90-year-old neighbour's shower fixed. One girl said, "Well, he could take a bath."

People were generally not allowed to see their new homes until they moved in. Badgering, though, got some people limited access. A 'Show Home' had been seen once. "It bore little relation to the actual bungalow," said Brenda. Pat Morris reports the relief he gave neighbours, showing them over his new bungalow.

John's words about their months of delay, living amongst packed boxes: "traumatic", "overwhelming", "consuming". His wife Gloria, already a stroke victim, became "rigid with depression".

"Go down to George Street Warehouse and make sure you get the carpets you really want," Pam is told. She is overcome with tiredness at the very thought.

She knows from neighbours the comparing of entitlements going on. (Allowances for carpets and curtains are graded, according to what people had before.) This is not the life she wants, the person she is.

Pam was conned by the curtain man: "If you give me £10 I can do this bit for you while I'm here.... It's not in the contract."

There needs to be a responsible person there to assist when the carpet or curtain man visits these elderly people, in order to see that they are able to pick a curtain and carpet that is suitable to the premises, and that they're getting a reasonable carpet and curtain. Some are getting better deals than others, and some of the old people are hesitant in coming forward. The carpet people are salesmen, the curtain people are salesmen, and we all know that salesmen are sharp. Elderly people are not. They may have been years ago, but as you get older you lose that sharpness, you lose that little bit of something to have a go at people, to say, no I don't like that, I want that. They take the easy way out....
Because as you get older you find that's the easiest thing to do. Unfortunately for some people, they think they're asking for too much, and yet they're only asking for something that's right and an entitlement. (Pat Morris.)

Pam's hassles are almost comically cruel. She was persuaded against her will to sell and be re-housed. They wouldn't believe she was disabled - tried to walk her uphill to a decant property. She had to pay for Medical Certificate proof. She was telephoned by the Trust to say her debts meant she could not qualify for the Homebuy scheme. Panic. She had no debts. How did they get hold of such (false) information? Address mix-ups meant her TV licence was challenged. She had power supply bills that didn't belong to her. Her own bills didn't arrive. Items are still in store, or missing, a year after moving in. Photos of her son's girlfriend were discovered to be circulating in the Works Office. The compensation offered for her garden is derisory. She's got to search through for invoices to prove her point. She hoped to take two young fruit trees with her. The workmen said they wouldn't survive. "They've got two chances," said Pam, going off to buy the tubs. They chopped the trees down.

Pam counts her losses: "The mature garden. The view. The

conservatory and extension and the light. It's like Cell Block H [here]." And privacy: "I have to be careful I'm dressed. My daughter-in-law can't breast feed in here." She's lost land, and convenient car parking space - cupboard space. Then there is the long 'snag' list...

'The Trust is running out of money.' 'Mrs. A got herself moved up a Phase.'

'The owners got first pick.' 'That couple are causing the delay.' 'You'll be Compulsory Purchased if you don't accept their offer.' 'The tenants on the Board get what they want.' 'Mr. B got £50,000 for his prefab.' 'There's no topsoil because the sub-contractors have sold it.'

Rumours are on top of people too. They are what powerless people say to each other. (My military service days were awash with rumours.) Work people started them, not wanting to show their ignorance, or wanting to reassure people, or wanting to scare them.

The strongest were the silent rumours: 'If you don't go along ...' 'If you complain ...' 'If you cause trouble ...' People fret themselves. The landlord can feel blameless.

Information was plentifully pumped out. (It could have been in bigger lettering and plainer English.) Uncertainties remained unavoidable: individual deals had to await each phase, plans changed as people moved on, changed their minds, died.

But rumours are really all divisive in effect. They take complaining pressure off the powers that be. Some of the main information is secret. At Newport the Business Plan itself is confidential. In the published minutes of the Housing Trust, after the heading, 'Finance', there are several blank pages. Rumour, then, is the collective, intelligent guesswork of people whose future lies in those blank pages.

Peggy (80) has been sent, twice in two months, 25 pages from the Housing Benefit department of the Council. They contain detailed calculations of rent, benefit and income changes. "What about the people who haven't got their faculties?" she asks.

Peggy is, like quite a few, claiming Housing Benefit for the first time. The higher rents in the bungalows make it necessary. But a fresh jolt this summer is the landlord's demand that disabled tenants must pay maintenance costs on their special aids. Peggy and Mary are faced with finding another £8 per week, and arrears of six months, because of computer error. "That's when your heart begins to race," says Mary.

In the time of promises no mention was made of these changes when tenants were invited to choose such aids as special smoke alarms and doorbells for the deaf. And there was no choice about special housing for 'scooters'. It was a legal requirement. The amounts for 'maintenance' seem excessive and arbitrary. It appears from the Tenancy Agreement (changed from a Secure to an Assured tenancy when transferred from the Council to the Trust) that the landlord can impose any 'service' charge it likes.

Mr Berry is being charged £3.10 a week to maintain his special toilet. And six months arrears. The toilet is wrongly installed and unusable during those six months. He has a commode provided by Social Services. He also owes on a bath hoist he can't use and a scooter housing and he doesn't have a scooter.

Mr Berry likes his bungalow. He has kept a remarkable view of the channel, and the ships entering the docks. But "It's the way these people treat you."

Compensation

Homeowners and tenants receive 'Home Loss Payments' when their homes are demolished. Owners receive 10% of the market value of their homes, tenants a sum fixed for many years at £1500. This was raised on the 1st of September 2002 to £3,100, and in 2004 raised again, to £3,400.

A number of Newport's prefab tenants moved before September the 1st 2002. (Some moved in that August, and received the lower rate.) Those who had borne the worst of the 'teething troubles' got least. The discrimination was, and is, felt bitterly.

At Penarth, the government saved its money. Clearing out people before a plan is formulated means their move is 'voluntary' - an ordinary transfer, and not compensated.

Monday morning, 6th December 2004

Janet's upset. She quarrelled with the heating man. He won't have it that the heating system in the new bungalow isn't working properly. ("Yet he's a nice man, by all accounts.")

Jack's upset. They've dumped an old chap in his new bungalow with no curtains, one channel on his TV, and little sorted. (Relatives or the Trust to blame?)

Penny's upset. Another stalling letter from solicitors about her claim. (She fell in the mud and broken pavement.)

Peggy's upset. Her crossness includes my failure to help. She's shaking visibly as she talks. Her new shower in the new bungalow has been mended three times and still hasn't been fixed. In the office the girls ask, 'Have you reported it?' Peggy imitates herself banging the desk: "Of course it's been reported. It's been 'mended' three times." They send a lad out. He eyes the shower doubtfully. "Have you reported it?" he asks.

Nothing new for a Council tenant, but Peggy's near the end of her tether. For a year, she's had her peat bags stacked up to stop her bedroom flooding.

But driving Peggy to the deep end is the lack of garden gates. Gates would keep out the dogs, whose messes are disgusting

Peggy no end. (We go hunting for the latest deposit.)

I have asked the Welsh Assembly Government why 'Security by Design' which has surrounded residents with high fencing, doesn't run to garden gates. And are residents' feelings about their own security taken into account? They told me to look 'Security by Design' up on the internet. There are several thousand references to wade through. The answer is 'No'. It's a police / architect thing.

Peggy voted against the scheme - never wanted to move. She collapsed, and they moved her husband while she was in hospital. Now the dogs do their bit.

Mrs. B's upset. (I haven't met her before.) "No, they haven't played fair." (She shakes her head. She's cleaning out her prefab. It has been full of smoke stains. The shed, and the just-empty prefab next door, were set on fire.

It was a lucky escape that the fire was spotted before it could spread to her property. She seems equally upset that neither the Trust nor the contractors, who visited the scene, called to see how she was.

Mrs. B. had challenged two boys about the place before the fire was discovered. "I'm not one who has a down on children. I've had boys..." These two rode off on bikes, shouting, "We'll ['so-and-so] kill yer."

Mrs. B's brother-in-law has finished helping her to clean up. On the scale of upset that day, he's top. He's too furious to answer my questions. "They've put more of our people in the cemetery than Hitler did ... They would never have had my vote if I'd known then what I know now..." His wife had died during their temporary stay in a bungalow, their 'decant' home. Now they want £100 off him. For his time in that bungalow. (Bungalows are rated in a higher Council Tax band than the Prefabs.)

They are pursuing him for the money. It seems this is an upset, an injustice, he can grasp. He can take these persecutors
personally. Refusing them, he is refusing the huge amount of
what has happened to him.

An average morning. I am not seeing the 'cup-half-full', the
happy, households.

'It's not them.'

"Mr. T. isn't the sort to swear. He's swearing now," says
Dave. "So are you swearing," Jane tells Dave. "Excuse my
language," says Janet. She hears friends swearing who have
never sworn before. Jenny, who knows her Bible, calls down
Old Testament curses on those messing up her life. Moira is
bursting to let fly, but can't overcome a lifetime's restraint.

Troops swear. Shocked and powerless people swear. And
moan. 'Sorry to be a moaner,' I hear most days. People
weren't formerly 'moaners', 'whingers', 'grumblers'. And they
weren't bad-tempered - though family, friends, workpeople,
officials, might come to believe differently.

Dave swears more, and smokes more, as Bristol's prefab
plans are being altered yet again behind closed doors.

People are being made into different people.

"If I had a gun I'd shoot the bastard and I don't swear"
(Mary).

SECTION FOUR

SOME PEOPLE

Nancy

Nancy has grown old today. I coincide with her return from shopping. I carry her bags from the door: "I can't do that again." Her leg is too painful to do supermarket shopping again. And it's getting more painful to use accelerator and brake.

Nancy's husband died. Alone, she changed her mind about selling her prefab and moving. She was threatened with Compulsory Purchase. "I didn't think they would turn nasty." It was two months, before furious campaigning won her peace.

On receiving the threat to her home, Nancy consulted a solicitor, at a cost of £180.50. I have been trying to get this repaid to her. It seems a landlord can threaten action against a home owner, forcing him or her to incur legal costs - then withdraw the action and punish the home owner (in this case Nancy) with the bill. The last response to my efforts to get the bill repaid is an angry dismissal from Edwina Hart, the Minister for Social Justice in the Welsh Assembly.

The thought, for two months, that she would lose her home, kept Nancy awake, and revived, in acute form, her ulcerative colitis. She seems to me to be more arthritic, too. (Nancy is in long queues for diagnosis, eye treatment, bathroom adaptations, judgement on her Attendance Allowance claim...)

Nancy's spirited conversations are a highlight of my Newport visits. Had she been forced to move, they wouldn't be happening. Nancy's prefab in the row of brand new bungalows represents to her more good times with her children, grandchildren, neighbours, friends, me.

One neighbour tells Nancy she should have moved. All commentators else have said they wish *they* could have stayed.

Janet

Janet's aorta valve now requires an operation. For a long time she has been advised that, with her other problems, such an operation could be dangerous. She is very frightened but, characteristically, 'getting on with it'. In the period before, during and after her move, she would be saying, "I can't take any more ... I'm ready to burst."

Janet had an immaculate prefab, 'La Siesta', done out in Spanish style. She can see it now, a blackened wreck burned by youths, across the road. Janet was prepared to move. She persuaded herself that a new brick-built home was an offer she couldn't refuse. I 'helped' Janet on the day of the move. I stood around pleading with her to relax, let the men do their job. The months of delays, hard negotiations over valuations, what she could take with her of fixtures and fittings, had changed her temperament. She is agitated about any marks done to carpets and furniture. Marks would be marks against her.

As Secretary of the Prefab Residents Association, Janet has been tireless on behalf of others. ("We've come out of people's places crying ...") Months after the move, she is fighting over the 'snags'. (They did mark the brand-new carpet.) My attempt at therapy now is to keep pointing out the view she has (compared with many), the light, the right choice she made of layout... They want to operate on the heart sooner rather than later.

Moira and Bill

It would stop this way of demolishing people's homes overnight if television viewers could see the lines of misery in Moira's beautiful face. And see Bill, in pain every day from his war wounds, smiling and supremely modest.

They were the couple I quoted earlier as praying to God to "get us out of this". Two years later, they are in their new bungalow.

I kept falling for Moira. At one residents' meeting the talk had turned to the mischief-making children on the building site. The strongest voices were saying how all had gone wrong since children couldn't be hit. Moira said to me quietly she didn't agree with hitting children. She had been hit as a child. "All it did for me was to make me shy all my life."

I learn now that Moira had collapsed the day before the move and remembered nothing of it. Seven months later, she is "95% better," Bill says. They suppose Moira had a slight stroke.

"I can't prove it, but so many have died," says Bill, letting the thought trail off. Many say it like that. Pat says it most directly. And Mr. Trees at Bristol. "Do you think people have died?" I ask him. "Oh yes, yes, yes," he says.

"We've lost the social," says Bill. He had wheel chaired round the bungalow roads, and seen one person. "Before, you saw dozens."

But Bill is making the best of it. He had been through D-Day and battles for the Rhine, and got his wounds two months before the war ended. He has shrapnel in his back, has had morphine prescribed for decades, has to rest up part of each day, and to visit hospital regularly for pain relief treatments. One arm is fixed at the elbow where he covered his head from the shell burst.

I'd like to ask if they feel they are 'owed' anything for Bill's war service. It's clear Bill doesn't. He can be upset by the neglect he knows some comrades suffer from. He doesn't watch the war on television. Moira does, "to see where Bill went." Moira says, with the only flash of anger I see from either of them, that the War Department lost Bill's records.

They tell me the story of trying to have a holiday abroad.

"Never again." Bill's shrapnel set off the airport alarms and they were grilled and humiliated over Bill's prescription drugs. Departments aren't in the owing business.

Moira is very far from settling in the bungalow. Every day is a reminder of loss. She is taking Librium again, last taken 40 years earlier, during an agonising divorce. "It detaches me." She apologises to Bill constantly: "I'm terrible to live with like this."

Moira seeks in the gardening what she had in her prefab. There are choices there. Her new neighbour is a great friend and gardening guide. Moira's armchair is planted to face the garden. A conservatory is planned, as a way of getting out of the bungalow.

Moira hates the new home. 'Frantic', 'desperate', are more appropriate than 'depressed'. She apologises to me for dropping out of the Residents' Group.

"I couldn't oppose anybody. I couldn't cope with people talking [their anxious talk]... They [the demolishers] have taken my sanity."

"Everything [after the move] was a hassle." The Site Manager was "rude" and obstructive when they wanted work done in the bungalow before moving. (Clearly a man who felt no sense of obligation to history.) They had two nights without a bed to sleep in, because they wanted to recreate their previous fitted bedroom.

The couple are Christians. It's with conscious guilt that Moira says, "I've become very disenchanted with people."

It's dawning on me that, with a bit of a fight, they could have emulated Penny and Nancy, and stayed in their prefab. They were told the land was required to sell to private builders. Bill, in his adaptable way, and Moira in her shy way, obeyed what they took to be orders. I can't say anything. They might be disenchanted with more people than they know.

Keith

Two days after catching up with Bill and Moira, I bump into Keith. As Chairperson of the Chartered Institute of Housing, he is an important influence on the Welsh housing scene. In the dismal story of under-investment in 'affordable' housing, and irrelevant policies, like stock transfers and ASBOs, Keith is proof-positive that shining characters and forces for good exist.

He knows the Newport Prefabs make me mad, so he opens up first.

He knows two women who work for Newport Housing Trust. He is most enthusiastic about them. One is a high-up. The other meets the residents. There couldn't be more caring people, he says. They have "come up like us." From the grass roots originally, he means, via college courses. They could only do right by people. "Yes, yes." I meet his enthusiasm with my vigorous agreement. I believe Keith.

SECTION FIVE

THEORIES OF NOT-CARING, OR CARING AS YOU CAN

INTRODUCTION

In this section I try to explain the rough treatment of elderly persons caught up in demolition schemes. Even in schemes that may pass for 'best practice'.

These analyses focus on the housing business as a caring concern, the powerlessness of the elderly, and the mentalities that initiate and carry out these plans. Media reports appear regularly detailing how badly the old are treated, as regards pensions and poverty, care in hospitals or homes, or as victims of crime and abuse.

It may throw light on the wider scandal to nail down a particular corner of it.

In its latest Paper on policies for the elderly the Welsh Assembly Government comes up with the need for a 'cultural shift' in attitudes to and treatment of the elderly. [19]

A CARE LESS BUSINESS

Some elderly people, forced to move from their homes, die as a result. They have been dying in this way for decades. Others will be in the next decade. Slum Clearance killed them, and 'Regenerations' are killing them still.

Doctors don't write this cause on the death certificates. Civil servants don't collect the statistics. Housing researchers don't use the word 'die'. What people say about their fate is only 'anecdotal'.

To present the evidence and make the argument, it seems necessary to explain what home is, and what ageing does. I may let people down by not doing that very well. With the mentalities at work here, perhaps I also need to explain what

---

[19] *National Service Framework for Older People in Wales.* WAG July 2005.
And see Appendix 5.

death is.

BAD OLD DAYS

In the bad old days I was a green volunteer in the housing 'movement'. Homeless families kept me awake, kept me feeling useful. People were dying then.

Mr. White died from a heart attack during an eviction. Slum conditions consumed their inhabitants. Damp housing and poor health were not connected - official. A young family couldn't escape from a fire because the windows were not designed to open wide enough.

These bad old days were in the middle of the great era of housing progress. The leap forward for working class housing, with the introduction of council housing after the First World War, was recharged after the Second World War.

Slum clearance was a huge rescue act. Urban 'regeneration' is to provide a 'Decent Homes' standard.

If the policy was hard-won and kind, hard hearts were necessary to do the business. The tide of angry, desperate demand always outran the supply. In my town, children with homeless parents were taken into care. Fathers, and boys over eight, were not admitted to Cardiff's Homeless Hostel. A key job for housing officials was to grade (and degrade) applicants for council housing, making selections for the better and worse estates.

I got excited when a death occurred. Mr. White's broken heart must make them think twice about evictions. (He was the father of several young children.) Seasoned social workers calmed me down. Deaths didn't stop the officials in their tracks. 'They' were covered. By the 'too many factors' cover, for example. Mr White was a sick man already. The coroner agreed. A death was proof of what people brought on themselves. Even, to their way of thinking, a source of satisfaction.

They smiled at us coming out of the inquest.

Punishment got into the official system of providing housing. One class was paying to house another class. Day to day, in the impossible job of making too few houses go round, anger is easier on the physiology than pity.

(The worst punishment housing I saw was a converted warehouse in Birmingham. Edwina Currie, as Chairperson of Housing, was setting out on a glittering career.)

Social workers, the 'bleeding hearts' department, were biased. They got at consciences that could not be afforded.

Some people relished the work. The little power was enough for some heads. Drawing blood or tears can seem a big power. Crying women are a regular feature of housing crisis. The manager couldn't help smiling as he held up his hands to show us the eviction was 'out of his hands'. The Director of Housing, comfortably retired, didn't bother now to hide his contempt for 'these people' - the tenants who paid his pension.

Power is a simple, and complicated, motive. These officials were tarred by the class they worked with. Contempt washes back on them. Some, maybe most, took the idealistic road, their part in progress. There are successful estates we should remember them by. And failed estates we shouldn't blame them for. But others used class contempt to protect their status.

Housing policy, decisions about investment, the supply of housing, are made elsewhere. The bureaucracy organises progress, puts the brake on progress, as dictated to. Kindness or unkindness gets handed down. It's a fact. It is the get-out clause for not caring, the cover of covers.

In the bad old days the slums were torn down too late, too slowly to save lives. The ravages of the Blitz had to be repaired. Both jobs were done in the post-war economic hang-over. No wonder, then, in that whole drama of competing need, upheavals of the old and vulnerable working class people could be overlooked.

But for those of us who saw the Mrs Murphys crying on their doorsteps, and the despair of the Thomases in the immaculate parlours of their 'Little Palaces', and didn't twig that a death sentence was being carried out, there is still some wonder.

BETTER DAYS

Pam, with a problem about her move at Newport, searched for officials from the Trust. She was told they were all off that day, taking exams.

It is different from the old days. Housing is a profession. There are potted plants and music in the offices. Help Lines and Advice Centres. Tenants are 'clients', 'customers'. The 'participation' of tenants and home owners on the estates and in regeneration schemes is the watchword - if not always the watch fact. Tenants' and Residents' Associations are encouraged, funded, trained. There are many more women in this profession now, and in higher jobs, if short of equal numbers.

There may be as many homeless families in this city now as in my green youth.

But those in the legally recognised category are taken care of much more humanely, by the designated Team. In the decision making and management of public sector housing, there would seem to be more openness, accountability, expectations of services and legal right.

The best new intentions shone out of those responsible for the Newport Prefab replacement plan. If the old school Director of Newport's Housing Department openly despised the idea of tenants' participation, the new Housing Trust couldn't have been more mindful of its public relations.

The original plan for Bristol's Prefabs showed that lessons had been learnt.

The boldest print spelled out that people could live out their days in their homes if they chose to. The choice that mattered. The pace of the replacement would be controlled by the residents.

The long burning crisis (from shortly before Thatcher) in the supply of public sector housing, came to break Bristol's housing budget. The kindness of the first prefab plan could not be afforded. The Director of Housing wrote his curt letter to clear out residents. The past hovers over the housing business: old mentalities revive as critical moments of supply and need recur. Proposals, now, to build plenty, build cheap, public sector housing exactly repeat the costly errors of the 1960s.

The past was alive and kicking in the Rhondda Valley. The blight of homes at Chapel Hillside lacked the intelligence of old slum clearance. Knocking down a home went with replacing it. The neglect in this scheme could only happen to the poorest families.

The clearing of the Billy Banks estate at Penarth was, it seems, to rescue people from the accumulated stigma. Concern for the tenants did not get them rehoused on or near the valuable land. Care for the rising land values overtook the show. New money beat new ways.

The new democracy worked best at Glyntaff. The active tenants and residents made this rehabilitation scheme more responsive to their needs. As at Billy Banks and Chapel Hillside there was only a scatter of elderly households. But even with the best scheme there was a degree of unrecognised suffering. One or two stressed-to-death people in an area of streets to be closed might be missed. But if whole populations of elderly and ill people, as in the prefab examples, are so easily, casually missed, the question of care is not a matter of oversight.

The punitive and hard faced history has gone. From most places.[20] Public relations and participation are here. Or nearly so. The keen and kind young ladies in the liaison role with residents at Newport would be much offended by my linking them to the bad history. Mad of me. They *are* their good intentions.

The Social Workers didn't entirely convince me. I retained my faith that if we showed people dying from a policy and practice, we were well on the way to stopping both. And forcing vulnerable people from their homes is such a policy and practice. It doesn't just upset them, confuse them, stress them, depress them, scare them, make their illness worse, temporarily or permanently. It kills some of them.

OLD PEOPLE POWER

Militant tenants' groups have usually won the most for their estates. Riots have won most money and attention. (Gains made, usually, at the expense of quieter, passive areas.) The much older Prefab activists, despite a demonstration or two, have not been able to sustain nuisance tactics and publicity-winning stunts. In Newport most were inexperienced in pressure-group working, moderately minded (at first), and almost all had the chronic conditions and disabilities of their age. The old are shy of conflict. Some of those who did rage probably hurt themselves most. ("It adds years to you," said Moira.)

Prefab residents were divided. Those needing to move, wanting to move, wanting to stay, tenants with no choice, home owners with no choice or too many ... divided by anxieties ... by the phasing of moves... We didn't have a bull's eye. We never centred on the killing facts. We never made the Trust, Council, Welsh Assembly, and all cogs in between, realise there were killing facts. The Mabel stories went whistling past their ears. Their perfect answer was not to answer at all.

---

[20] A recent discovery in a time-warped (i.e. poor) Welsh valley: Blaenau Gwent Council still carry out house inspections. One inspector had a particular relish for dictating to single parents about tidiness.

Dave Drew in Bristol learned the facts of power. Councillors have less of it than officials. Specialised, technical sorts of knowledge carry the day. Everyone is covered. Officials and councillors cover each other. The Council is covered by government policy. Contractors and consultants join the dance of 'partners'. The bottom line is now Bovis's.

Bright sparks like Dave and his campaigning friends can learn and be effective in all the machinery of government, to an extent. Resolute triers like Janet, Chris, John, Jacqui, at Newport, can protect some people some of the time.

"If I had money I'd get out of all this," says Mary. Others say the same. Powerlessness is poorness.

> Middle class home owners win territorial battles against roads, hostels, gypsies... Or don't get bothered in the first place. If need be, they can back political pressure with legal challenges. No one has been able to afford any legal defence of a prefab, or other cleared homes. No home owner has so far had the nerve to hold out for a Compulsory Purchase hearing.

> Mr. C. might. He is looking up the ins and outs. He has found this: "Compulsory Purchase law is unnecessarily complex and its procedures archaic and tawdry" (the Law Commission).

Sections of the Human Rights Act seem to have been written to protect people from just such extreme impacts of public policy, but it costs money to prove it. [21]

(Talking of law: Anti-Social Behaviour Orders (ASBOs) are made against persons who cause others to experience 'alarm', 'harassment' or 'distress'. We see some individuals paid well, and promoted, for causing just these things.)

I learnt, as a caseworker, that political power is not uncon-

---

[21] For Human Rights Act, see Appendix 10

nected with physical power. Alongside a woman and her children, I might persuade an official because I was fit, male, six foot tall, and weighing 15 stone. And I could do educated talk.

I did feel like hitting someone when Mrs P. was bullied by a contractor's man.

In reply to a complaint, the Trust described the incident as Mrs P. 'refusing to talk to their representative'. She had turned away in fear.

The power played out in this little scene is instructive. The bully, perhaps, doesn't know he is bullying. He doesn't know what Mrs P. has been reduced to over months. The letter writer from the Trust is covered for the lie: the old are unreasonable; all this is for their own good. 'Regeneration' is one big cover.

But then perhaps the man is pleased to see Mrs P's fear. He has had a bad day, a bad contract, a bad life. Mad by deadline and margin. Or perhaps they are all just dim. No answer acquits anyone. In their stressed state, prefab residents could contrast their lack of effectiveness with ethnic minority pressure groups. Immigrants were listened to, got what they wanted The women's movement forced the inequality of women into a great many consciousnesses. The concept of the inequality of the old is yet to arrive. The pensioners' vote is beginning to feature at election times. Pensioners' organisations are forming. Some are marching. They haven't economic leverage, but might find a political one.

Age Concern and Help the Aged knew what I was saying when I approached them with prefab stories. But they couldn't back up. They seemed blocked by the same politics and mentalities over a much wider range of issues. Their roles as charities and support agencies preclude sharp campaigning.

The majority of residents, in these examples of demolitions, are council tenants.[22]

Once, local Labour parties and Labour Councils were their strength and shield. Once many more Labour councillors were themselves tenants, and even a few MPs paid rent.

(It should be noted that the author of the first, kindly Bristol prefab plan was herself brought up in a prefab.)

But home owning has become the priority for all political parties. The 'ladder', the mortgage interest rate, the booms and busts of the market, hold the headlines and trigger the nervous systems of the elected representatives.

The next-to-nothing of Council tenants' power is nothing for elderly tenants.

From a distance, creating new homes is the 'community' fully caring. Whatever the limits of budget and print margin, material, skill and time are being invested in the present and future old. There's proof. After her weary months in the prefab home Brenda declares her bungalow "lovely". "I absolutely love it," she says.

Jacqui explains the care-lessness that hurt the people who didn't love any of it. "It's because they don't live here." The people in charge and the people on the receiving end are not the same people. Every public sector home is decided upon by people who live in the private sector.

Britain provides the poorest pensions in Europe. geriatric medicine is the lowest-funded medical specialty. The old are 'bed blockers'. You smell the statistics in care homes. The

---

[22] This will not be true of the demolition fervour in the 'Pathfinder' and 'market renewal' programmes in the North of England and the Midlands. Pam, Ken, Moira, prefab owners at Newport, will say owning gave them little power.

For 'Pathfinder' details, see Appendix 9.

scandal that refuses to surface. Doing the rounds to place a relative makes a bureaucrat of you. You compartmentalise the experience, hand responsibility over, create your own cover. Death by demolition is a fraction of what does for the old. A local denial, hidden in a huge one.

Housing stories, upset residents, are the daily bread of the local press, radio, and sometimes television. Publicity is a power that the prefab residents thought might save them.

Knocking down prefabs did attract journalists. In comparison, schemes at Penarth and Tonyrefail, with their slow attrition, were small beer. The special features at Glyntaff - first transfer of Council housing stock in Wales, etc. - got more attention.

The Prefabs battle at Bristol even appeared in some national newspapers and on BBC Radio Four. Prefabs had their historical link with the War and its aftermath. They could stir memories of a time of collective endurance and feeling. And then there were these very quaint aspects. Against the odds, some prefabs were still with us. And lots of people did not want to leave them. A little interviewing turned up the fact that these prefab sites were examples of successful communities. The elderly inhabitants valued the settled neighbourliness. Qualities that often eluded new built estates.

The journalists went for these little ironies. The Prefabs made good photographs. With an 'old folk' standing in the doorway. What we didn't get were the deaths and damage to health of the demolitions. The coffin coming out of the door.

Editors need proof, and rightly did not want to scare. But they were not about to investigate our arguments. There were occasional stories. An argy-bargy between the residents and the Councils, Trusts... The editor of the Bristol paper gave good coverage to residents' protests, and then declared itself 'neutral' about the proposals. Such media do not want to be on the wrong side of 'progress', 'regeneration', 'redevelopment', the future... the promise of money for the town.

We perked up in Newport when BBC Wales decided to make a film about the Prefabs and the new bungalows. We all believed in the power of television. This was to be a proper programme, not a one day wonder in the evening paper. *Palaces for the People* (the nostalgia note from the start) explained the history of the Prefabs, and then followed two elderly couples through demolition and re-housing.

Two vivid scenes completed the film. One couple were shown gobsmacked when they first went into their new bungalow. "Is this for us?" they stammered. "Do we deserve this?" Music to the Trust. The other couple showed, in their trembling, their fear of the whole process. Their happy ending was to open a letter from the Trust which told them they could stay in their prefab. Everyone a winner. Good 'feel-good' television.

I had badgered the researcher for the film. Could they show people being made ill, dying? She was friendly, concerned, sympathetic. She 'knew what I was saying'. But that wasn't their 'brief'. That wasn't the programme they were 'commissioned' to make.

The story for BBC Radio Four's *You and Yours* was: Bristol's Prefab scheme bad, Newport's good. Bristol's plan (then) scattered the Prefab people. Newport's kept people on their sites. The programme may have helped swell the protests in Bristol. It buried us again in Newport.

John told a BBC journalist of his Newport experience, "If I thought I had to go through that lot again, I would go down to the Transporter Bridge and hang myself." That sound bite never sounded. And none of mine. The neat, save-the-community story could be told in no time. The mortal story would take a little longer. The media, in these cases, 'win us with honest trifles to betray us in deepest consequence.'

The bruised face of a battered pensioner stares at us from the front page. Slower muggings don't show.

Journalists have told me that council tenants aren't 'sexy'. The thrills and spills of house price booms and busts, the money, does it for them. With so many persons and things commercially and competitively sexualised, the old are the last to get a look in.

Media power is real power. At Newport it may have got responses to complaints and solved an individual's problem. Coverage at Bristol, together with the local campaign, helped change awful Plan B to better Plan C.

Demonstrations at Tonyrefail won some attention, and maybe shortened the agonies there. The sheer number of demolitions planned in Northern England in the 'Pathfinder' programme is producing resistance and therefore media concern... [23]

The Chairperson of Newport Housing Trust is a councillor with some prefabs in her ward. She is an excellent worker for 'her' people, an impressively fair minded server of the public. She is determined to make a success of the prefab replacement scheme. (My frightened friends curse her with the rest. But the point is the good intention and the real ability.) I stated the case (at the Chairperson's invitation) that the old and ill are profoundly stressed in such upheavals, and that some should be left alone. She stirred with annoyance. Didn't she know all that? She was up to her neck in everyday helping. She lived with these people and their problems. Most needed rescue from obsolete, unhealthy prefabs. She, the Trust, had won a big vote - had ample backing from the majority of residents. (Some of this 'backing' was seated around the table. The Chairperson was restraining their verbal attacks on me.)

I said that some of the elderly people were frightened - they

---

[23] Radio Four's important news programme 'The World Tonight' has carried more detailed items about the Pathfinder demolitions. We have had the missionary zeal of the developers, the don't-want-to-go voices of residents, the progressive architect talking of the need to consult and compromise. The only 'deaths' are those of 'communities', and of 'old terraces' that "have had their time".

were scared of the Trust - so no one knew what they really felt. At this the good Councillor and the Trust officials actually bounced in their seats with anger. They were tremendously insulted. I was saying they frightened old people.

Fears I knew of from Council estates included: victimisation, if they went against the Council; exposure as illiterate; exposure as a 'fiddler' of benefit; exposure as inadequate; exposure as being afraid...

In the Prefab clearance case, fears include: of conflict; of 'causing trouble'; of not understanding what was being said; of doing the wrong thing; of losing out in the re-housing; of what rumours meant...of what stress was doing to them, to their partners .. I had thought I was stating a fact of life, known to all of us in the 'community' business.

So the good Chair and senior officials took it personally. They were seeing themselves, I think - their energy, goodwill, pride in making things better. And with the proof they had, around the table, and up the road... How do you see past yourself? The scheme they managed had to be wholesale. Against exceptions. They could make it work.

Two years later, the Chairperson forbade me to make any further contact.

I had written an angry letter charging her with responsibility for causing hardship to a distressed couple. The Trust had threatened Claire and Colin with eviction and homelessness. They were refusing to take up the bungalow allocated to them. It did not fit what had been agreed between them and the Trust. Any delay threatened the sale of land for private building - a key part of the plan's finances.

The couple - much younger than most - had serious physical and mental illnesses. Claire was described by her GP as having the worst nervous condition of all the 10,000 patients on their books.

The private building was the issue between the pair and the Trust. At the last moment before their move, plans showed that these homes for sale would overlook and crowd in on the allocated bungalow. One of Claire's conditions was claustrophobia.

When the row broke out, Trust officials told neighbours on the site that delays were due to this couple's actions. A simple, useful, lie. An official complaint extracted an apology but, of course, the damage was done. After several months in their new, unwanted, home, Claire and Colin asked me to stop campaigning for them. They would try calm.

Six months later Claire, in her 40s, died of a heart attack.

I am with Mrs P. She's had a phone call from the Trust. Someone will visit her. Nothing to worry about. She *is* worried. 'Why are they coming?' she keeps asking - and I keep reassuring.

Mrs P. chose to stay in her prefab, and fought off threats of Compulsory Purchase. (Her story was told earlier.) I don't think her health has been the same since - but who is to say?

I arrange to be with Mrs P. when they call. Two lively young women arrive. Does Mrs P. have any problems? That's what they've come for - to see if she is all right.

I suspect, with Mrs P., that there's more to the visit than meets the eye. And probably more than meets these young officials' eyes.

(New bungalows are to be built on either side of Mrs P.'s prefab. There could be boundary issues. Complaints from another stayer-put have been upheld by the Welsh Assembly. Is Mrs P. going to be trouble?)

We respond to the young women and their eagerness to please. They do light up the place. They are here to give people the right information; there are so many silly rumours. The latest is the silliest. We urge them to tell us. People are saying that land allocated for new bungalows has been sold instead to the posh hotel up the road.

I should have lectured them on the truth of rumours. How they grow in the dark. Measure fear of the future. How they are especially fertile in the last years of these long-term programmes. The main fear is that the money is running out. People have experienced changes in the plans and delays. There are signs of economy: the small print under the early promises becomes the big print. On another site, eight prefab residents must leave that area. Land there has to be sold to private builders. There's nothing silly here.

On my own with the officials, I explain that Mrs P. is very nervous. Oh yes, they know. I really don't need to tell them. That's their job. Worry is their element. Hence their cheery manners.

I don't think they know Mrs P.'s 4.00 am wakings, the library book reading until dawn. All started up again by their phone call.

"What was all that about?" Mrs P. asks when they leave. She is more suspicious than before. The Trust is covering its back, I tell her. They want to know in advance if she'll be trouble. Mrs P. sits back in her armchair. Cynical explanations are the true ones, she has learnt from her long work experience. And they are not after her home.

Watching Mrs P.'s body relax into her chair, I realise that she has been a lot more frightened than I knew. This is the point of this story. I have been calling regularly for nearly two years. I am writing the book on fear and trembling.

I want to use what's happened to her. I've delved into it. I have watched people knocked over with a feather, a harsh word from a workman. And I still don't get to the bottom of the fear here. How powerless Mrs P. is against her fears. (I don't live here, either.) She really thought they were coming to take her home from her.

Mrs P's fear is life damaging. I see that it is deep in the way people have to leave power and politics to others.

Mrs P. is alone. Two together are more than double the power of one.

With more care, the old would have more power. More sleep, stronger bodies, more confidence in the world's good nature.

It's been sad today. Instead of being frightened Mrs P. could have enjoyed the liveliness of the young company, its natural tonic.

The old don't riot and cannot strike. The insecurities of living through housing crisis mean people are easily divided. A hard history has conditioned the providers of public sector housing. The complications of government baffle and divert the opposition, and spin out the process for weary years. There's no money to try legal defence, or to fight effectively, or to flee altogether. The political party of tenants has gone elsewhere. Caring, without back-up, is wearing. The whole scandal of the last years of many old people when it surfaces refuses to stick in the collective consciousness. The nation, talking to itself through the media, is in more interesting conversations.

Give everyone an extra vote with their pension. I did think two-vote people might change the see-saw!

But there was the potential democracy in our grey and balding heads, round the tables and in the meeting places, to keep people alive and well through these plans. It needed to be the beginning, middle and end of them. We have to see why it cannot be that way.

IMAGINATION - LACK OF, THEORY

Dying at 80 is less tragic than dying at 60. There is not the same alarm or curiosity about causes of death in the elderly. As Shipman taught us.

There is a natural revolt, an immune barrier, against imagining our own last years. Who wants to know failing body, faltering mind, loss of those we love, the multiple non-choice of possible deaths? Our imagination serves us by stopping short. And, by extension, steering clear of others' ends.

'Ageing is a slow surprise', said someone in the know. Age comes on 'stealing steps' to 'claw you in his clutch'. Shakespeare put the terror into it. Spared the details (if we are lucky) of our end, we can spare ourselves the imagining.

'They are too young.' 'They don't understand us.' 'They ought to have older people coming round.' 'They don't listen.' 'They're graduates' (Brenda). Sayings from Newport.

But quite elderly officials, councillors, politicians, took decisions and saw their impacts on the residents. Power must keep the imagination young.

The imagining required to save the Mabels and the Moiras is to put yourself in their place; 'Walk a mile in their shoes.' ('Walk a mile in their moccasins', is the Native American advice.)

It is difficult imagining. Being a stranger, in another skin or gender, is against the grain. And a mile is a long way.

If nature sides with us against the old, not to be them before our time, we would also not think of being the weak and unequal. The effort to be 'ourselves' takes us in the opposite direction.

Janet, John, Gloria, Bill, Jacqui's mum, David's mother-in-law, are among the disabled. Perhaps only the disabled know the disabled. The mile in the wheelchair especially long. Dependency is another dread to defeat the imagination. The disabled muster cheer to fend off pity, pity which means to be at the mercy of. Perhaps the disabled have daily to strive against self-dislike. And we are, maybe, all too busy trying to get on with ourselves.

People facing clearance could feel they were treated as objects. Units of less value than the land. A piece of the map. In someone's career. A point of profit. The public meetings, the half-hearted forms of 'consultation', could reinforce the individual's sense of powerlessness. The platforms were not imagining the feelings of the floor. They had plans for them.

Tenants at Tonyrefail were reduced to look like objects in their passivity and mute anger. The look that says you can do anything to them.

People imagine differently. Scientists and artists fire from different corners of the brain. There's 'good at things' and 'good at people'. Picture-people see changing places, objects modified, the world made over. Story-people see the people in their places, attached to their things.

The planner's imagination is already in his brief and on his drawing board. The imaginations of architect, engineer, builder, banker, manager, are on the job. 'We see what we know'. The actual lives they are changing can be a blank, and probably beside the point. The imagination is divided by separate spheres of responsibility and work, with little or no remainder.

I always come away from Newport cursing the National Assembly of Wales. An architect friend came away cursing Le Corbusier.

Le Corbusier's architectural imagination became that of a whole movement. An economical fashion was born, which included a solution to mass producing workers' housing. A well intentioned imagining. For the people, if not by the people.[24]

The imagination that goes into producing the homes and the places also goes into shaping, limiting or expanding the imaginations of the people living in them. My friend the architect was seeing the limits of imagination. Fifty years on from the Prefabs, here are more extensions to look-alike-bungalow land. Solutions for the car and 'security' accentuate the individual isolation.[25]

The Prefabs may have been clever Le Corbusier. Designed simply and functionally. But offering big advances for many working class people - fitted kitchens, bathroom suites, generous gardens. And now adapted by decades of living imagination.

A comparable advance now might build places to give the old a better time and demonstrate how we might live with them in more solidarity. (The Community Centre in the Newport plan is shelved. Residents demand CCTV to protect them.)

This is not to blame the particular architect. Their brief is made up from resources available - densities laid down - catering for the car. But the stale architecture that results, and the unimaginative treatment of the people, come from the same stable.

Janet is doing battle with Newport's Planning Department. In their imagined plan she has to have a hedge and a tree. Janet's home owning always meant she decided her own garden. Facing major medical treatment, she is desperate to imagine low maintenance. The angry exchanges (the last of many) aren't helping her defective aorta valve. Hearts are needed to imagine hearts.

A theory of not-caring might go: to imagine other lives, and perhaps care about them, you have to see them in some detail.

---

[24] Le Corbusier. Swiss-born architect, 1887-1965.
[25] See Mike Fleetwood, 'Goodbye to the Prefabs', *Touchstone* Magazine, August 2004

Class (ever at the back of housing policy) can't see, won't see, sees what it wants to see. The official isn't allowed to see. Work people see their work. Budget, deadlines, profit margin, fill the horizon. But over and above and inside these realities there is an indelible mentality at work. A mentality that skews what is seen and heard. And translates what is immediately seen and felt into something else.

A mentality, an outlook, comes with the fact that we live in generations.

So much thought, feeling, imagination, is bound up with our peers. Their lives reflect ours. Those in different phases of life cannot count for so much. 'They'll get over it,' dismisses the frightened old and the hurt young. (In truth, seniors and juniors have immeasurable power over us. But our generation tells us the results, and tries to tell us how to live with them.)

I am trying to excuse the failure of my imagination. I saw, spoke with more desperate people, probably, than anybody else. Why didn't I see those dying of despair? My encounters in the slum clearances of Cardiff, Swansea, Newport, coincided with my first steps in a political career. Excitement clouded my view. So much of my attention was caught up in the doings of Party bosses and colleagues.

It is more or less the same mentality of the generations that overrode Pam's hesitations, decanted George and Jenny, dismissed Carole's doctors' letter ... didn't see what Mrs Murphy cried about in 1965, or Mabel in 2002.

The impatient mentality defeats the good intentions of the politicians and the planners. But they will still celebrate their good intentions. Bungalow land will open with flourishes. No stop over at the cemetery.

Our mentality, with enough other things equal, is to cherish all life while it lasts, and in memory after. Grief the greatest pain. (So many, let down by the human forms of life, pick up on the pets and plants.) We are 'bound each to each in natural piety.' To have a secure 'identity', the modern formula for happiness, for all its 'selfy' sound, is always to do with accepting others and being accepted by them. And, selfishly, we can calculate that our care to come will be better for others' now.

Death and dying insist on being imagined, for all the distractions and tricks we get up to. Too much imagining looks like too little. We get a global fill of suffering.

It's the wearing and wearying that cuts down on sympathy. 'O that's sad,' people say, when I buttonhole them with the miseries of Mabel and Murphy, having to slide around another sharp little reef. And with no charity box to square the thought. Emotions stop, or lose their force and meaning, when no action is possible. People saying 'They'll get over it' are, perhaps, hoping for themselves.

But we would have to say there is more imagining of others now than ever before. More tolerance of minorities, more convergence of feelings, more democratic manners, more education and information. We can afford people more. There are more elderly people to think about. More getting disabled rights. More living alone. More people imagining themselves, walking the same miles.

The cruelty displayed toward the old and ill in demolition schemes, the refusal to hear their protests or consider evidence, is less to do with an all- pervasive mentality, than with a particular mentality bred in a particular business. The power relations (who chooses), the ways it has to make its money are deep dyed habit.

In the 1980s I got caught up in Council tenants' 'Action Groups'. They were formed on the deprived ('disinherited' Jean used to say) estates in the towns and valleys of South Wales. Together we worked up an exciting head of steam, with demonstrations and sit-ins. Getting the houses up to standard, people got up to standard. The challenges to local power changed the passivity of lifetimes and released all kinds of personal aspirations. The increasing awareness of political realities, of how the world worked, was especially an imaginative revolution. The lifting of the individual's horizons was a condition of lifting everybody's. The same boat held all the inequalities.

The lesson is that imagining is not simply what our brains can do for us, what some people have more of than others, part of a job description, but a gift that is lost and won. The callously dim saying, 'They'll get over it,' and the passively puzzled saying, 'He never got over it,' are among the defeated.

Our 'Action Groups' ran into the buffers, Thatcherism, Blairism ...

Our time isn't a good one for the collective boat: horizons are being privatised.

King Lear is Shakespeare's play about the forced house moves of pensioners. The ex-king is 'decanted' from ungrateful daughter to ungrateful daughter. From the highest rung on the housing ladder he falls to sleeping rough. He can't make it out: "Is there anything in nature that makes these hard hearts?" he cries. Pam, Moira, Mabel, Mrs Murphy, couldn't make out what was happening to them.

The unkindness makes Lear mad. He had ruled blindly. Now he can catch glimpses of how wretches live, and what injustice does. He begins to "see feelingly".

Perhaps a feeling theory of care awaits us when age has clawed us into its clutch. Imagine the theory now, and we may still have some power to put it into practice.

CARING AS YOU CAN: THE THEORY

We are at the Welsh Office. Checked through security and ushered into an impressive committee room. Six tenants from the Welsh Tenants Federation, and myself as advisor. We are enjoying the promised 'access' to the new Welsh Assembly Government.

'Stock transfers' is the subject of the day. The Government's policy to transfer council housing to new landlords. Newport's Prefabs will feature. They have been transferred to a not-for-profit Trust for the purposes of their demolition and replacement. It is the first transfer in Wales under the new rules. 400 down, 200,000 to go.

The young men from the Housing Section at the table are familiar. But the senior Civil Servant in Wales also arrives. What's this? Do we really have sticks to put in their policy wheels, or mud for their eyes? Perhaps he needs to check that the juniors give nothing away. The Labour-run Assembly had tried to get Wales exempted from the Transfer policy. But the Blair line, to be done with Council housing, refuses to recognise the Welsh border.

Central to the transfer policy is the choice tenants will have. They can vote 'Yes' to the new landlord on offer, or vote 'No' to stay with the Council. Since Councils are prevented from investing in modernising homes or new building, a 'No' vote is a vote for run-down. So the choice is a cynical pretence. And perfectly on a par with the vicious financial discrimination perpetrated against council tenants by Thatcher and Heseltine.

We discuss. We point out that the homeowners at Newport lose their homes but have no vote. Home owners who exercised their 'Right to Buy' will be caught up in regeneration schemes. Top man gives his scribes the nod to check this out.

The 'Yes' vote at Newport is promoted by an expensive PR campaign. It's not fair, I'm saying. The tenants do have independent 'advisors' provided for them. But Newport Council turned down all 16 recommendations they made.

In my stride, I illustrate the PR tricks, the ad men style. The Trust's Newsletters serve up the promises in warm colours, and smiling pictures. Possible snags are relegated to back corners, printed in unpleasant brown. Top man laughs heartily at this. He is tickled. He doesn't look as if he gets many laughs at work. He shrugs across at my simplicity. "It's a competition," he explains.

His laughing loses me the thread. I fail to ask about his, and the Minister's, roles as referees. Isn't there some duty that way, the 'level playing field' stuff? Evidently not.

This is a tip-off from the top. It's a competition.

Joan, Mary, Ken, Bob, myself know we are up against no less than the Government. Backed by the not very strong muscle of Tenants Associations scattered across the estates. But we had in our heads that something like a dialogue exists, and the possibility of persuasion. 'Don't bother', the man is educating us.

And coming away from the offices, we realise the game we played was lost some time ago. When the ideals of public sector housing were abandoned by the 'modernisers' in the Labour Party. When the electorate voted in too many Conservative governments. When the deals were done to make the interests of finance and land, property development and contractors, sure-fire favourites. We are among the 'also rans'.

Down the road, Jenny and Janet, and over the bridge Dave and Daisy are losing heart to the regenerating teams of public and private parties. Mabel competed with her crying and lost the lot.

My prefab friends are shocked twice. (Were shocked twice). By losing their homes, and by their powerlessness. 'Powerless' doesn't just mean 'weak' or 'vulnerable'. It means losing.

In fact, the people in these schemes are barely in the race. Almost all the competing goes on before it gets to them. Housing consultant versus consultant. Contractor versus contractor. Banker versus banker. Career versus career. So many competing for their own corners, ambitions, securities, long lives. People minding their own business. Mabel and Moira are a side show. The fearful residents are up against a massive attention deficit disorder.

And this is what the people from Newport and Bristol are saying, very sadly or very angrily; 'we're beat' and 'they don't care'. The theory of not caring is first the powerlessness and second the indifference. The double life of inequality.

We are all supposed to be better off for the competition that goes on in all these property, land and finance markets. We are bowled along in the official theory, and this official can laugh at us today. He knows better than us; it's all going to be all right in the end. Or as good as all right as can be. Planners have to be sharp winning the job, builders about beating rivals, bankers about doing the deal. Clients and customers come out well...

But Mabel, Carol and co are not customers or clients. Governments and Councils buy these plans for them according to priorities, cost limits, lobbying... Mabel and Carol may be 'stakeholders' in the jargon. With lives at stake, they hold least. When I argue to Assembly members, Councillors, planners, officials, that the terrified and ill should have a 'Right to Stay Put', a special silence falls. It is a definite danger that those to be demolished should have a stake, should be in the game.

[We won the headline today. Criticisms of Newport Housing Trust. Prefabs left empty scare the neighbours as they become targets for thieves and fire raisers. The landlord will be going home to kick the cat. Our turn to be happy that they aren't. (I should correct that. They want us to be very happy, but become defensive/aggressive when we fail them.)

It can't last. A few days later they have a full double page: 'Prefab scheme is a model for others.' It's the Director of the Trust talking. A happy customer is shown toasting his brilliant new home. It's put together with a propaganda piece for the transfer of all council housing to just such landlords.

The spinning of untruth, you realise, is the absolutely necessary accompaniment of today's political and economic competing. It's got to be win, win. Bedraggled losers not allowed on stage. The air of unreality must be pumped into the space between our ears. What reality do they live in, the vanishers of Mary and Mabel? Do they stop their competing when they close their front doors behind them?]

I nearly always see eye to eye with my Newport friends. But when they say, 'No one is listening,' I have tried a political lecture by way of explanation. The Welsh Assembly hands powers over housing to Councils. Tenants voted for the Trust to take powers from the Council for the 'regeneration'. Government (London) policy sets it all up. What my friends are caught in are crossfires and passing bucks.

There is a democratic sense to it. Sharing decisions between centre, region, town. Checks and balances. Even our wise man at the Welsh Office is a lynch pin making it work.

'They are in it for themselves,' my friends say, to my lecture. To feel as defeated as they do, the force against them must be raging self-interest, if not actual corruption

I don't know if their political theory is more accurate than mine. They are too exposed and I am too protected. Democracy has to be a competition for the ruling jobs. The disasters of demolition happen off the political map. Usually in a few homes in a town. It's an issue that promotes or demotes no politician.

Very few politicians (or anybody else) may be entirely 'in it for themselves'. But power is a current you get stuck to. The good they would do competes with the competing they have to do. They are turned away from my friends.

The man can see the joke while we are telling him tragedies. To climb to the top of his tree so he can measure the Whitehall trees above him, he must have competing much in mind. But he is giving us the goods. The democratic 'deficit' is not that some are 'excluded' as their jargon goes. They are defeated.

It is a forgiving theory. We are all competing at bottom for bread and safety. More or less openly and desperately, with or without luck... We can't be minding out for everybody. We might see the rubble and the bulldozers at work and wake up to a different landscape. But we don't see far into the complex, specialised making of change and 'progress'. We need life to be in compartments so we stand a chance ourselves.

The man's theory, 'It's a competition', helps to understand the people.

We can be surprised, when some criticism does get through, at the really injured tones, the very thin skins of those in charge. And how urgently they run for cover. It turns out they are frail competitors, awaiting the results of their careers and lives. But dangerous, because deaths don't stop them. They feel their own lives are light and forfeit.

There are the completely complacent. With a total ease of con-science to every distress in front of them. They have already won. Occupy a safe place of power. Place themselves in the right class. The losers are before them that they need for proof. There are a few downright cruel. So curt and cold to the old and disabled as to be taking revenge. These, one guesses, lost earlier, are marked by abuse and humiliation. For them the old and even the dead can never be powerless and must be chal-lenged to give back what they owe.[26]

Most workers in the field are the well intentioned. Surprised, if they are honest, that the happy ends in view turn out mixed results at best. Disaster at worst. They don't know what they

---

[26] People bent on cruelty can be enraged by pleas for mercy. The victim is manipulating their emotions. Perhaps the helplessness of old and ill produces in some degraded persons similar reactions

are up against. See the awkward customers, not their own awkward place in the scheme of things.

The Civil Servants' theory persuades me to rethink my descriptions.

The man I wanted to punch for bullying Mrs P. wasn't a bully. A Contractor (and all who sail in her) has to be a competitor and a half. The man of action was mashing his gears to get down to the old woman in front of him.

And 'lack of imagination' is more clearly the thoughtlessness that comes from having too much to think about. Competing in the skull.

[Bristol Council demolished some perfectly habitable prefabs just when it (they) were looking for temporary homes for nearby prefab residents. "Yes, it was a mistake," the senior official admitted freely.

Every public utterance of the Council people, since we hit them with the evidence (collected here in Section One), has had the word 'sensitive' in it. This 'mistake' pushes people all over the city and lessens their prospect of ever returning to their old ground. What were they, the Council people, thinking of? Their heads perfectly empty of thought? Or too perfectly full? Or this official is having us on? Another bout of demolitions is a score to them? It breaks resistance.]

There are too many of us, I guess." Dave the tireless campaigner is on a downer. He is losing the argument in his head. What can his prefab neighbours expect?

The numbers on the waiting list for homes in the town are scary, as they get thrown at him. The numbers of homeless likewise. Some of his neighbours are coming up to say the immigrant numbers are scary.

There are 'too many of us' for the supply of affordable homes because Thatcher and Heseltine knifed council house building two decades ago. Too many homes were deliberately unbuilt. Housing budgets fixed for needs to exceed supply. Dave and co. have to compete with old defeats. It is exhausting for the bravest spirits.

The face to face hostility amongst neighbours at the Newport sites has been especially painful. The Residents' groups for and against the scheme, or its methods. Conflict no one wanted. My friends struggled to be tolerant through the nerve-wracked years. And doubtless the other side did too. With health often failing, tempers failed too...

In the Welsh tenant's movement we became horribly familiar with squabbles amongst ourselves. "There must be someone up there with a great big spoon stirring away." Winnie used to sigh.

Those failures of solidarity on the council estates are a complicated story. Some spoon there. The stirring of the 'regeneration' pot is easier to see. It is not difficult psychology to grasp how vulnerable, fearful people can be set against the other. How the pressure from above produces the sideways cracks.

Working with Tenants' Associations on the estates of South Wales over three decades, one observes the 'sharp end' of so many Government policies. In 1989 the Tories withdrew benefits from school leavers. (And reduced benefits for 18 to 25 year-olds.) It was a most damaging blow for young people and their families. (The coming of drugs in a big way, and then guns, dates from this time.) The tax money saved benefited the better off. Clearly a well thought out result of the Conservative theory of competition and caring. We are all better off for the richer being more rich. For the youths cast adrift, as for our pensioners now, the same puzzle arises. Did the Tories know what they were doing? People are being eliminated by these policies. Do they know? Do they know, and do not care?

The theory that economic competition is good for all, for all time, is founded on rocks of denial. It's nice because it allows its promoter to know and not know at the same time, care and not care.

Youths roam the building sites and bungalow roads. These early losers find weak opponents to scare. Their defiant look says what our man said: 'It's a competition.'

"You can't afford this fight." I'm telling Penny. With her blood pressure soaring, she is doing battle over her borders. She has kept her prefab. She reckons the bungalows going up around her are taking strips of her land.

I insist her health is more important than a few inches of land. Penny snorts back at me. It's not the garden, nor her health. She has to take them on, on principle - the principle being that they won't eliminate her. They will not take her for nothing in this life. She will make them care, even if it's cursing. Penny has watched the personalities of defenceless neighbours dwindling. Losers stand to lose more than their lives.

Research shows that people die of inequality. Over and above direct causes of premature death, like poor diet and disease, lower class, lower status, lower rank people die before their 'superiors'. Penny is determined not to die of shame, or whatever it is that kills the unequal. She may join the statistics by another route.

Edwin Chadwick in the 1840s, kick-started welfare reform. Crucially, he got the law to enter causes of death on certificates. Perhaps it's time to enlarge our science as to causes of death. Allow on certificates 'Home Loss', 'Policy', 'Avoidable Stress', 'Fear', 'Inequality'.

Penny is feeling better. She seems to be winning. The contractor's men are visiting regularly to discuss the work on her fences.

A competition competition. Penny is better treated because:

(a) An earlier complaint was decided in her favour;

(b) She is visibly more disabled now;

(c) These are decent blokes, coming to the end of a difficult contract;

(d) Frequent meetings are bringing knowledge of each other's problems. A co-operative spirit is born;

(e) A mix of the above?

There is care. The landlord at Newport, when stress levels could no longer be ignored, called in a Tenant Support Team. This is a paid-for, means-tested service, for tenants only. John, Peggy, swear by the kindness of these 'strangers'. It makes you think how a little in the way of running errands, hospital lifts, form-filling, goes a long way with these elderly and disabled clients. Who knows what saves a life?

More people are paid to care. It's a growing vocation, profession, business. (Care Homes are traded on the Stock Exchange.) Counsellors and therapists are coming off an assembly line. Lawyers get work arguing the 'duty of care' owed, or not owed by public and private bodies. 'Care' is injected back into a system that's squeezing the natural stuff.

(Parents paying others to parent for them from 8.00 am to 6.00 pm is the most striking example of our times. Putting our old people into 'care' has become second nature.)

Paid-for care puts it into the competitive frame. It is underpaid, often under-trained, in our neck of the woods. It can be brilliant. It can be non-existent.

Costs are rising even for those on the lowest of incomes. (Home care charges have more than doubled in Bristol in little more than a year.) The new bungalow tenants in Newport face big bills for their disabled adaptations.

[Jenny is reeling from a letter claiming she owes £80 in arrears on the maintenance of a disabled toilet she has for her 92-year-old husband. After the awful years and the new home they dislike, this is the last straw. When are the shocks going to end? She is thinking about sheltered housing. (The first line in every Welsh Assembly policy for the elderly is the commitment to support 'independent living'.)]

How do we care in a business-like way? The government, as in the Health Service, believes that more and more competition between suppliers of care is the modern answer. There is no idea in the heads of government that co-operation, solidarity, kindness, could work and be rewarded. And that, as our example shows, there is enough competitive fear in lives already, to make them past caring.

'It's a competition.' The man was saying, it's the way we live now. The political and economic arrangements we know, vote for, and have to love. It is the best possible cover for inhumane acts. 'Not me, the system.'

But the indictment has specific charges. The housing business is a regular crisis, burying most of its tragedies. The lesson it relearns are the value of land and property. Divided work divides responsibility. Ignorance lives at all levels. Age, disability, death are most difficult to work with. To know what progress is, you need to know what happened in history, and why good intentions aren't enough. People in their own lives are too fragile to know fragility. Solidarity under strain won't stretch over the generations. Care is what can be afforded. Denial survives. Imagining doesn't.

And the Mabels, like the Murphys go down quietly, unseen. By the by to the democracy we can believe largely works for us.

Brenda speaks for how many when she says she loves her new home? Dave speaks for others: "It's murder, really."

As a socialist I knew, before the man said, that the competing world loses us everything that cooperation would win. John Ruskin wrote 150 years ago, "Competition is the law of death. Co-operation is the law of life." It's the life and death match I've been watching at Treberth and Stelvio, Horfield and Ashton Vale...

As they would say at the boxing, 'One for the loser'...

Too many have passed away already. We do not need any more to pass away. Kick the bastards out of office now!!
How dare they try to take away my house that has been in my family for 57 years.

*It affects everything, every day. It is criminal really. But our lives are on hold. This is taking a chunk out of our lives, in fact. How can this be humane? To keep people dangling, not knowing what to do or what is going to happen. It takes any pleasure we may have **away**. It dominates everything - our thinking, everything!!! !! It is CRUEL.*

We want to be left alone in our friendly and quiet place.

SECTION SIX

A RIGHT TO STAY PUT

RIGHT AND LIFE

Proclaiming a Right to Stay Put got me funny looks from every official and professional. I was not a serious contender.

Clever dicks start in: 'What happens... you get one stayer in a block of flats about to fall down?' And 'The road (or runway) will create thousands of jobs, make life safer... Staying-put householders make change impossible.

The rare case condemns the common one, by people who have no idea how the sentence is carried out.

The sincerely puzzled say homes do become obsolete. 'Unfit for human habitation' can be a scientific test. It harms people to stay put - even if demolition does harm. In practice, (Newport Prefabs) this reason to get people out is used not to think about harm at all. All's well that ends up with new property.

The first, kindly, plan for the Bristol Prefabs gave people the choice of staying put. Unfitness came second to the wishes of residents. Patch and mend would keep the places as safe as possible while people lived.

But this 'right' was a promise to be broken. People's peace, their need to stay put, were pitted against the needs of the housing queue in the town. The budget allowed no Right.

The kindness was a policy, not a Right. Three different policies in three years drove 70, 80, 90-year-old people on a sickening roller coaster. Some couldn't hang on for dear life.

Nancy, Penny, a few others, have stayed on in the prefabs they own at Newport. New bungalows surround them. This took some doing. Threats of Compulsory Purchase were in the air. (In an actual letter, in the case of Nancy.) But none have been used in Newport. A CPO would reveal the iron fist in the PR glove. Televised weeping would have won our case.

At 'consultation' meetings in Bristol prefab owners were told directly that Compulsory Purchase would be used against resisters. And resisting tenants would be evicted.

People were made ill by these meetings and threats. How many sleepless nights followed, how many unhappy decisions were taken, is of no account. A Right accounts.

Many homeowners were shocked to find how little right their owning gave them.

But the few who managed to stay are homeowners. And the Compulsory Purchase process itself offers a chance to mount a defence. It is a thin chance. Appeals against Compulsory Purchase come late in the day. Plans are long laid. Finance arranged. Alternatives ruled out. Contracts often signed. It's the person versus 'progress'. The petty claim, against the town's prosperity.

Tenants have to go willy-nilly. Not even the thinnest defence. No necessity for the Council to prove its case that the home can't be made fit, that the communal good is at stake, that no alternative plan is possible.

Medical evidence, whether people will survive or no, would go with the Right.

And become the first consideration in any process that demolishes homes. Everyone has to sit up to it. The big people and the little people meet on equal ground. And the machinery between them is laid bare.

With the Right, tenants at Tonyrefail could not have been shifted about for years with no rehousing plan on the cards. The poor would have had a stake.

With the Right at Penarth, owners and tenants could have bargained to return to their attractive site. Made sure promises were kept.

At Glyntaff there was a virtual right to stay put. The Council tenants voting 'No' to the transfer to the Housing Association remained with their Council landlord, and out of the rehabilitation and demolition scheme. Since then, the Labour government has abolished this right of the 'No' voters. [27]

The prefabs of Penny and Nancy stand out in the neat lines of bungalows. An irritation to the planners, and an inconvenience to the contractors. 'Sore thumbs' as progress. But life saving, maybe. With the Right from the start, beyond argument, these women would have been spared the insomniac intensity of their campaigns. And Moira and Pam wouldn't be inconsolable now - and others wouldn't be dead.

The law on Human Rights includes the Right to a Home.[28] There was no money to test out whether this might mean a right to keep your own home. The public might have valued the argument: what Nancy, Penny, Moira and co. called a home, and what others called it for them.

The Right would not save everybody. The old, faced with 're-generation', will worry whatever. Ken and his wife could have stayed in their beautifully modernised prefab. They were on the edge of the site. But what to do for the best for their families - prefab or bungalow - bothered them for years, and aged them.

---

[27]   Every Council in England and Wales has to consider transferring its housing stock to new landlords. Under the pressure that the Council itself cannot borrow to invest in its stock. New landlords are a variety of 'not-for-profit' organisations that can borrow from the private market. Tenants have a vote to approve the transfer. In several striking examples - e.g. Birmingham, and Wrexham in Wales - tenants have voted 'No', throwing their councils into disarray about their future ability to look after their stock. Where a majority do vote 'Yes' to the transfer, the 'No' voters, under Labour's rules, have to accept the new landlord. Whether these costly semi-privatisation benefits tenants is hotly debated. Transfers do not automatically means regenerations and demolitions. In most cases it simply means a new name on the rent card.

[28] The Human Right to a Home. See Appendix. 10.

Elected governments cannot guarantee any absolute Rights. Circumstances and votes change them. For the crunch cases a process is required - any proposal to demolish homes that intends to override the residents' Right to stay put should be tested at an independent public inquiry. The medical evidence, and what people say for themselves, would be first up. Among the competing interests, life itself. Such a process, applied to Newport or Bristol, would have saved lives. It would make people feel they exist. We would know exactly what we were doing to this person and that, and for whose good.[29]

There could be crunchier cases: neighbours versus neighbours. The majority, wanting new bungalows at Newport, or resigned to their inevitability, were frightened by those dragging their feet, apparently spoiling everyone else's chances. That was the set-up. All must go with the majority vote. The awkward squad, with the Right to Stay Put, would have been a different proposition. A group of tenants could have been massively more reassured, more honestly negotiated with. The plan could have been different, as most plans can be.

Dave in Bristol lives with his partner's acute fear of having to move. They worry about the outcome for her 87-year-old mother. He knows the distress of all their neighbours. Faced with these distresses, Dave sprang into brilliant political life. He, more than any individual, brought about Plan C from Plan B. Instead of scattering all residents over the city, new bungalows will be built on almost all the prefab sites.

Dave knows there's plenty of misery to come. The anxiety of the when and where. Two moves or one. Working out the money. The end of peace and quiet. And the lesson of the last few years is unmistakable: it's a job for the Council and Bovis, not a caring one.

Dave's suggestions include a medical and Social Services team assessing every individual need in the threatened housing. The attempt to work out what 'community' means in each area.

---

[29] See Appendix 11, the case of the Tryweryn Dam

Building to be done by local firms instead of the giant contractors.

It is the best list of wishes. I think it will remain so without the legal force of a Right to Stay Put. Dave retains, I think, the idea that just about everyone could be moved safely, given proper knowledge, support and compensation.

It is not possible to get people out of the path of the economic, political, historical bulldozers without the recognition and force of legal right. A kinder mentality will not take root without that. Nothing else will penetrate the complacency, the interlocking shields of irresponsibility.

Dave will go on tirelessly saving people. I am pie in the sky. I have had to give up the idea that we could save lives at Newport. We will see (if it can be seen) how many go down in Bristol in the next five years.

Once political reformers and revolutionaries aimed to create a State that would take things off the rich to give life to the poor. And growing state power was available to clear slums and build more equal cities.

Today, the owners and controllers of economic wealth are as safe as their several houses. (And the servants of the state enjoy bountiful security. Bristol's Director of Housing's recent pay increase of 15% represents a couple's annual pension.) The same cannot be said of the Newport, Bristol poor-in-power. Nor of the isolated old caught up in the 'Market renewals', the 'Regeneration' now in force across Northern England.

Taking homes has been democratically done. Replacements built and compensation paid. (The replacements that failed, the story of the 'estates', is completely relevant to our case of not-caring. And the £60,000 homes promised by Mr Prescott make it seem as if the 1960s disasters never happened.) The methods have marked us off from the mass carting off of the population by the totalitarian regimes of our time. The individual had, and has, rights, if not the one to stay put.

But the force experienced by Jacqui, John, Janet, Jane, is totalitarian in effect. It has totalled many people in the last decades. Those who hate their new homes - Mary, Moira, Peggy, Pam - have had their lives dictated to.

The use of state power to make unequal people more unequal - as in ill, and dead - is an irony. Another might be that this conservative demand, the Right to 'stay put', could be amongst the more radical of our time.

The defenceless old could be as safe as the rich. 'No entry' posted to the 'partners' and bureaucrats. Tenants equal to homeowners. Socialism with individual guarantees. Solidarity as the cornerstone of planning. Imagination the light of architecture. In the age of anxiety, the local identity reaffirmed. 'Help us, somebody.'

APPENDIX

Appendix

Contents

Appendix 1

Prefabs

The Prefabs were a post-war emergency response to the housing crisis. Housebuilding had stopped during the war. Many thousands of homes had been blitzed. 157,000 prefabs were built with £150 million from the Government.

There were several types of construction (Alcon, Phoenix, etc.). With baths, indoor toilets, fitted kitchens they were, for many, a big improvement over previous housing. They were meant to last 10-25 years.

Scientists recruited from the war effort designed the prefabs. Perhaps no other housing for working class people has ever had such brains at its service!

'Demolishing the Elderly' is about demolishing the homes of all sorts and doing harm to their occupiers. It was the concentration of the old and ill in Newport and Bristol that brought about the campaigns and this study.

The prefabs would hook the media for a one-off piece, which invariably missed the killing point. E.g. Guardian headline, 'HOME IS WHERE THE HEART IS, EVEN WHEN IT'S A PREFAB' (Jan. 19, 2004). This over a sympathetic account of the Bristol arguments.

156

Appendix 2 (i) The Kind Plan

Allocations   Bristol Council Tenants' Newsletter, March 1999

There are a number of options for the residents of prefabs:

	Option	What you need to do
1	Remain in your prefab	Decline opportunity to complete transfer request.
2	Move permanently to a new bungalow on the same site.	Confirm in writing that you will not wish to return to your previous address, once it has been redeveloped.
3	Move temporarily to a new bungalow on the same site and, where possible, return to your former address once redeveloped.	Confirm in writing that you will want to return to your current address.
4	Move permanently to a new bungalow on a *different* site.	Confirm in writing that you will not want to return to your previous address once it has been redeveloped.
5	Move permanently to an alternative type of housing, away from the site.	Confirm in writing that you will not want to return to your previous address once it has been redeveloped.

Under option 5 , only tenants with young children will be considered (as a priority), for a move to a house. Other tenants can be expected to be considered (as a priority) for a property with no more than two bedrooms (for example, a single occupant of a prefab can be considered for an alternative two bedroom property).

The important point to stress is that *you do not have to move out of your prefab if you don't want to.*

Appendix 2 (ii)

The Unkind Plan

Bristol. July 2003

Please ask for: Nicky Debbage or Alison Napper
Telephone: 0117 9664605
Fax No: 0117 9531340
E-mail: nicky-debbage@bristol-city.gov.uk
Date: 09 July 2003

IMPORTANT - THIS CONCERNS THE FUTURE OF YOUR HOME

. Dear prefab tenant/ owner

I am writing to all prefab tenants and residents of privately-owned prefabs to make you aware of the councils' proposals for the remaining prefabs

As many tenants are aware, some of the existing housing stock is becoming difficult to repair and replace with the money we have available for housing repairs. The council also has a very limited amount of land to make available for new homes which are badly needed by the whole community.

Whilst the remaining prefabs are popular homes, they can no longer be repaired and need to be replaced. However, continuation beyond next summer of like for like replacement of the prefabs is no longer possible. The recommendation to the council's cabinet is that prefabs should be replaced with more homes, and a wider mix of type of homes, in partnership with a developer. No redevelopment is likely to happen for 2 years, but the plans will mean that the sites will be redeveloped within the next 8 years.

We are aware that this is not what you may have hoped for. All remaining prefab tenants will be offered priority for rehousing to alternative council housing, and help and advice to move. We will also look at ways of involving private owners affected in plans for the site.

We understand these proposals may raise a lot of concerns and queries. Therefore we have planned a number of public meetings, and the nearest one to you is at Ashton Vale Community Association, Risdale Road on Thursday 24th July 2003, starting at 2.00pm.

If you have any questions before this meeting please contact either **Nicky Debbage, Technical Strategy Team Manager,** on 9664605 or **Alison Napper, Policy Officer,** on 9664601.

TUES

The recommendation is to go to the council's Cabinet meeting on 15th July, at 10.30am in the Council House.

Yours sincerely

Ian Crawley Director of Neighbourhood and Housing Services

Procurement
Zion House
Coronation Road, Bedminster
Bristol BS3 1AN

Ian Crawley
Director of Neighbourhood
and Housing Services

Website
www. bristol-city.gov.uk

Appendix 2 (iii)

Bristol's Plan 'C'

After the Director of Housing's letter cries of outrage went up and a campaign started.

This forced the Council to adopt (what I am calling) Plan C.

The deal, explained in the text above, allows Bovis to build houses for sale on the prefab sites in return for building bungalows for the Council.

This proposal was hailed by the Council as a 'great day' for prefab residents.

In practice screws were put on half the prefab owners to sell to the Council under threat of Compulsory Purchase. And the delays in drawing up detailed plans and firm commitments to tenants is clearing them out by attrition.

18 months after the appointment of Bovis, no contract has yet been signed (promised for six months hence).

197 prefabs have been vacated between the Director's July 2003 letter and December 2005. Most residents have been transferred out to 'elsewhere in the city'. Some 30 have gone to sheltered accommodation and residential care. An accurate figure for deaths is not available. When the replacement bungalows come to be built in the next five to seven years there will be few of the original residents living in them.

Dave, Mike and others call these plans the 'Don't Know' plan. Because that is always the answer they get to specific questions about their future.

Mr. and Mrs. D are moving out before they strictly have to. Mr. D fears he might die. He is in poor health and does not want his wife to struggle through the upheaval alone.

June 2006

The contract with Bovis promised for last year is still not signed. More delays, more anxiety, more 'don't know'

Meanwhile the number of properties Bovis can build for itself has more than doubled (731 from 314) since it has won the competition. Bungalows for the Council are reduced to 197. The promise to rehouse prefab residents in bungalows is now 'as far as possible'. As is the promise for former residents to return to their communities. The profit motive is galloping away with peoples' hopes. Partners they are not.

160

Appendix 3

PLEASE TICK BOXES BELOW   Age 70

1. Which Prefab site do you live on   HURFIELD

2. How long have you lived in your home   27 Years

3. Are you –   Tenant ☑   Owner ☐

4. Do you worry about what is happening to your home

    All the time ☐   Most days ☑   Not Much ☐

5. Is what is happening causing you Health Problems

    Yes ☐   No ☐   sometimes

6. Is it causing you Stress

    Yes ☐   No ☐

7. Is it making you feel Depressed

    Yes ☑   No ☐

8. Is it effecting your Sleep

    Yes ☐   No ☑

9. If you already have a health problem, has it got worse

    Yes ☑   No ☐

10. Have you any other COMMENTS about what is happening

    It seems they are hitting the older and
    infirm the most by this decision. They made a
    point to put us all here and now will cause a
    lot of distress plus ill health maybe a way
    of killing us off   J Gibson

PLEASE TICK BOXES BELOW Age [7 7]

1. Which Prefab site do you live on _WALTON RD_

2. How long have you lived in your home _58_ Years

3. Are you — Tenant [ ] Owner [✓]

4. Do you worry about what is happening to your home

   All the time [ ] Most days [✓] Not Much [ ]

5. Is what is happening causing you Health Problems

   Yes [✓] No [ ]

6. Is it causing you Stress

   Yes [✓] No [ ]

7. Is it making you feel Depressed

   Yes [ ] No [✓]

8. Is it effecting your Sleep

   Yes [✓] No [ ]

9. If you already have a health problem, has it got worse

   Yes [✓] No [ ] _CANCER_

10. Have you any other COMMENTS about what is happening

    NO COMENT

    CANT

Bristol Prefab Preservation Group Survey, Autumn 2003

This questionnaire was sent out to all tenants and prefab owners after the Director of Housing's letter cancelled the option to stay in their prefabs.

Appendix 4 (A)

WAG Housing Research Report, May 2003

The Implementation of Social Housing Clearance Programmes and their Social Impact.

1.1.   *The scope and purpose of the study.*

1.1.1.   *This is a report of a literature review carried out by HACAS Chapman Hendy for the Welsh Assembly Government to examine the ways that social housing clearance programmes have been implemented over the past 30 years in Britain, in order to see what impact this has had on tenants. Specifically the review aims to:*

> *identify how residents have viewed the clearance process, and the nature of their involvement in it*

> *and*

> *explore the impact of social housing clearance on specific groups (particularly the elderly and vulnerable household) and identify best practice in consulting residents*

The report lists 56 research papers, Government documents, surveys, etc., dating from 1971 to 2002, on the subject.

But comments (1.3.3): *"During the course of the literature search it became apparent that there is very limited evidence dealing specifically with the effects of demolition and rehousing in Britain over the last 30 years ..."*

This is, in fact, a useful statement. Compare with this reply from the Minister for Social Justice and Regeneration. She was replying to our descriptions of very upset old people:

Whilst it is recognised that there will inevitably be negative factors associ-

ated with any redevelopment we have to balance that against the body of evidence which demonstrates that poor housing contributes to a range of physical illnesses and that housing problems generally can impact on people's mental health. The research also points to evidence which indicates that residents who were rehoused on medical or social grounds experienced dramatically reduced levels of anxiety and depression after the housing intervention and a striking improvement in their self-perceived health status. It also suggests that investment in housing improvement can add value by reducing the health, crime and education-related costs associated with poor housing. (January 2004)

The Minister is a lot more certain than her own research. She is missing the actual matter of the Mabels and Moiras. And talking to them isn't evidence.

In spite of the Report's stated scope, direct references to impacts on the elderly are very limited, pack no punch.

is frequently the case that those affected by demolition and redevelopment plans are among the most vulnerable, disadvantaged and socially excluded members of society. This reinforces the case for ensuring that where social landlords are considering or delivering programmes involving the demolition of people's homes, the needs of those affected are at the forefront of their concerns."

The consultants well know how many other concerns are competing for the forefront.

But they do edge a little closer:

"Nevertheless, as the literature reviewed for this study demonstrates, decisions about the benefits or otherwise of demolition are rarely straightforward and even against the backdrop of a comprehensive regeneration programmes and effective resident involvement, demolition can have unforeseen or unwanted outcomes."

'Unforeseen', 'unwanted'! Do they mean the death word? Why don't they say the death word?

Appendix 4 (B)

The Minister's letter referred to in Appendix 4 was the most forthcoming of the replies received to the many letters, reports etc. we sent over five years.

The Minister understands the 'stress and anxiety' involved in such demolitions. That's why the Review (Appendix A above) was commissioned. And why extra money was provided to bring in the Resident Liaison Officers. And why the Tenant Support Team was also operating. The lessons of the 'insensitive' clearances of the 1960s and '70s had been learnt. (Tell that to Tonyrefail, Billy Banks, Penarth.)

She reminds us again of the overwhelming vote by residents for the transfer. The Minister ends up, "It's hard to see what more we can do."

Exactly which lesson is it that the National Assembly of Wales has learnt from the '60s and '70s? Janet, Mabel, Ken, Moira, Mary... are the lessons.

In defence of Wales: the reply from Whitehall to our letter about the Bristol demolitions implied with cold condescension we had neither the knowledge nor intelligence to teach them anything. (This from Nick Raynsford's office. That man once a hero of the little people fighting the London developers.)

Appendix 5

'Joined-up Thinking'

The vocabulary is striking. A collection from five years' Welsh Assembly Government documents relating to Health, the Elderly, Social Services, Housing, ontains multi-agency', 'inter-agency', 'cross cutting', 'corporate', 'holistic', 'flexible', 'thematic', 'co-ordinated', 'integrated' ... .

The bureaucracy is clearly in a fierce wrestle with itself.

The latest invention is of special interest. From *National Services Framework for Older People* (WAG July 2005).

"The achievement of this vision requires a cultural shift placing greater value on old age and older people and new ways of working at all points along the integrated care pathway, from prevention of dependency and ill health, to timelier intervention and support within a whole-systems framework."

The sermon on a 'cultural shift' to value old people is coming from the government which decides the economic and political 'shifts'. And the shifts of housing policy in particular. But note the 'whole systems framework' and the 'integrated care pathway'.

Friends in the business say that strides have been made in really working 'thematic' committees between local and central government, 'partners' and 'stakeholders since the Local Government Act, 2000, set up the requirement to draw up 'Community Strategies'.

A fly in the ointment is that as housing gets ever more privatised it need not join the dance. It is more joined to the system of markets than such committees.

Simply, before the jargon hypnotises us, putting health foremost would directly scupper the 'regenerations' described in this book.

It comes down to Bert. Aged 80. Bert has to pay to have strip washes and baths. Bristol Council refused to install a walk-in shower in his prefab. In its mind it's a condemned property. In fact Bert has years of strip-washes behind him and years more to come. To have the necessary help costs him £40 a week. A housing official expressed surprise at this amount. His mind not at all joined to his own Council's Home Care charges, and not at all to the indignities involved.

Our knack of thinking is how we join up the world, make sense and meanings. The calls from the offices of government, fed by professional and academic thinking, to overcome its own departmental divides sounds increasingly desperate. For in other offices of government, and out here, the 'thematic' force is the value of competition and its ways of thinking. Ways which 'cross-cut' the time and trouble we have for our fellow citizens.

This is the analysis, this is the reason for not-caring, offered in Section Five.

The blinkered practices in housing and in services for the elderly do have to be comprehended in a really whole 'systems framework'. The planet needs its 'integrated care pathway'.

Bert's housing officials, 'culturally shifted' to think beyond their immediate jobs, would be aware of his plight. For Bert not be in a plight requires the politics and economics to shift.

In July 2006 W.A.G. announced the intention to appoint a Commissioner for the Elderly.

Appendix 6

In 'Living in Wythenshawe', Doreen Massey returns to her family's council house home. She has become an academic authority on places, 'spaces', and economics. She writes about how people make their cities and are made by them. In the article she describes her old locality from the viewpoint of her mother in her wheelchair.

These are some of her ideas that fit the Newport and Bristol experiences. (Some 'translation' from the academic has been done.)

"Changes in the ... environment may tell you that your time is passing."

"... picking your way through a world now increasingly made by others."

"The mirror held up by the modern city reflects to many elderly people an image in which they don't appear."

"The ways places are changed make it harder for elderly people 'to look out for each other'."

Or even look out and see anybody out there, which is what Ken, Bill and

Mary are saying...

Appendix 7. Newport Housing Trust

Helpful Guide to Moving House

Four weeks to go

- ☐ Check your home contents insurance policies to ensure that you are covered for the move and at your new address
- ☐ Notify British Telecom and ask them to make necessary arrangements for final account/transfer any services e.g. deaf facility at your present address and for installing telephone facilities at your new/temporary home
- ☐ Arrange for change of address cards
- ☐ Notify your cable/sky installer and make necessary arrangement for final account at your present address and for installing at your new/temporary home

Two weeks to go

- ☐ Confirm all arrangements, times etc
- ☐ Begin to throw out unwanted items from attics, wardrobes, what you really do not want you may as well dump now, or send to charity, it is a great time for a good sort out!
- ☐ Arrange for automatic redirection of your mail by the post office

One week to go

- ☐ Send off change of address cards
- ☐ Cancel and pay up accounts for routine delivery services such as milk, groceries, newspapers, fuel & pop. Re-organise these deliveries for your new address
- ☐ Make arrangements for pets

One day to go

- ☐ Complete your packing (if applicable to you) that you have agreed to deal with yourself. Except for those items you are likely to need overnight and prepare any meals necessary for moving day
- ☐ Have enough cash to deal with unexpected expenses and make sure you have collected documents and valuables together in a safe place
- ☐ Check through previous lists to make sure nothing has been overlooked - then enjoy a worry free early night!
- ☐ Empty refrigerator and deep freeze and defrost interior
- ☐ Pack personal items to take with you including jewellery, insurance policies

Moving day

- ☐ Strip beds and pack bedding and nightclothes
- ☐ Pack items for washing/toiletries

- ☐ Take down curtains
- ☐ Take up rugs, carpet/floor coverings as required
- ☐ Dismantle any light fittings etc
- ☐ Turn off electric appliances
- ☐ Disconnect cooker
- ☐ Turn off boiler/central heating
- ☐ Turn off water
- ☐ Read gas and electric meters
- ☐ Secure all windows
- ☐ Lock all doors
- ☐ Leave keys with builders/residents liaison officer
- ☐ on arrival at your new home, unpack slowly and methodically so that you can check for loss or damage

Extra Hints for a smooth move & who to notify

- ☐ Pension, Bank / building society
- ☐ Post office
- ☐ Insurance company (house/car)
- ☐ Gas/electric/water board - (by Lovell on moving day)
- ☐ Telephone company (BT, Sky, Cable)
- ☐ Local authority (council tax)
- ☐ **Driving licence authorities**
- ☐ Inland revenue
- ☐ Store cards and accounts
- ☐ Other lease, hire or rental companies
- ☐ Employer
- ☐ Doctor/social services/community nurse/meals on wheels/home help/hospital/chiropodist
- ☐ Dentist
- ☐ Schools
- ☐ Professional bodies/trade unions
- ☐ Motoring organization AA/RAC/CSMA
- ☐ Newsagent
- ☐ Organization, clubs, magazines
- ☐ Newsagent
- ☐ Friends and relatives
- ☐ Library (return books on loan)

Important items to take with you

- ☐ Important telephone numbers
- ☐ Insurance policies
- ☐ Medicines
- ☐ Clothing & food (to carry through the day if there are any delays)
- ☐ Personal items for your first night in your new home

Appendix 8

Living on a Building Site

From a letter to Newport Housing Trust

Dear Sir

I write to you with Regards to incidents that have occurred over the Period of Starting Redevelopment in Drinkwater Gardens phase 4 & 5

1. The constant Dust and Condition of the Road.
2. The Parking of Vans, Trucks, Cars, and plant, on Pavements Resulting with Everyone having to walk on the Road.
3. Constant Blocking of the My Private Parking Space That was provided for Disabled parking
4. The Placing of Two Cement mixers. Right next to the Parking Space Resulting in Constant Cement Dust Being Deposited on My Car Every Day.
5. This was brought to your attention at the Gathering at the Newport Centre.
6. The Cleaning of my car at the car wash, Every Friday. With an Estimated Cost of £120-00 with still more visits expected.
7. Every Day use of water for various reasons around these Mixers, Resulting in the Parking bay and the Path to 47, and 49, being flooded with cement contents, Mud etc.
8. If this was not enough the Road Sweeper. Was depositing its Load at the end of the Day. Right next to the Mixers. Around this period of time the Weather was Not Very good. So Along with the Contents of the Cement mixers, and the Road Sweeper, the bay and path was in such condition that we had to have it hosed Clean.

9. The Depositing of Earth to such a Level out side 47 and 49 also resulting in Flooding of Both of our Gardens. Leaving mud deposits all over the Path and Steps. These also had to be hosed down.

10. The Site Manager was Notified of these Problems.

11. The water being used at these cement mixers was being transported by the green Machine on pallet in a blue container, and then the blue containers were Moved closer to the Metal Fencing, and a hosepipe was dangled over the one Fence across the path and over the other fence. These were left to fill For well over one hour with water running all over the place.

12. At some time. With the Fence being moved for the road works, and the Moving of the Containers. Ropes holding the Fence Secure were removed.

To try and set off the Cement Dust being deposited on my Car, a Green meshed Sheeting was erected and was secured to the Fencing, this did help a little but the Dust was still getting through, with my car still having to be cleaned.

Mr B. continues his letter with the account of how his car was damaged by the badly secured fencing. He has to scurry round for repair quotes. He is without his car through the Christmas period.

He signs off:

> "I am amazed that myself and my neighbour, have had NO visits from anyone at Trust to see how I was coping. When we are living on your Building Site. I have reported problems by phone, and even spoken to you about them and still no visits. I suppose out of sight out of mind might be the quote."

Appendix 9

The 'Pathfinder' Programme

In February 2005 Deputy Prime Minister Prescott announced a £500 million 'market renewal' fund to regenerate areas of towns in the North and the Midlands where "the problems of low-demand housing and abandonment are most acute."

The nine schemes are in North Staffordshire, Hull and East Riding: South Yorkshire, East Lancashire, Manchester and Salford; Merseyside: Newcastle Gateshead: Oldham, Rochdale, Sandwell (Birmingham).

Three additional areas were allocated £65 million in March 2005. Yorkshire and Humber region: North East and North West regions. The Pathfinders come under Mr Prescott's strategy called *Sustainable Communities: Homes for All*:

"The schemes will entail over a 10-15 year time-frame radical and sustained action to replace obsolete housing with modern sustainable accommodation, through demolition, refurbishment, and new building."

These 'regenerations' have the clarion good intentions of the former 'slum clearances'.

Rescue may indeed be at hand for many in these rundown places. Though criticisms can be made about the strategy here and some individual schemes in particular.

(The too little, too late again; the too few affordable homes now, and to come; the too little democracy, the private partners leading the 'market renewal' will narrow the choices of Councils and residents; the private interests will require large scale clearances to make it worth their investment ...)

Newspaper reports tell of 'tens of thousands' of demolitions.

The point for this book is to register how baldly 'obsolete' and 'demolition' are set down. (Doubtless 'sensitive' will appear all over the prospectuses.) There is no recognition (even in the statements of opposition groups) that demolishing the elderly can find them the path to the grave.

Appendix 10

The Human Rights Act, 1998

This law starts promisingly for our case:

(Schedule 1, Part II, Article 1):

'Protection of property: every natural or legal person is entitled to the peaceful enjoyment of his possessions .... '

(Section 8):

'Everyone has the right to respect for his private and family life, his home and his correspondence ....'

Then it falls away: the qualifications of the above, in order, are:

'There shall be no interference by a public authority with the exercise of this right except such as is in accordance with the law and is necessary in a democratic society in the interest of public safety, economic well-being ... or the rights and protection of others'

and

'No one shall be deprived of his possessions except in the public interest ... 'and what the state decides is the general interest.'

It giveth and it taketh. One can see in these words there may be scope for a courtroom argument against unwanted demolitions. So far there has not been the money to get there.

Appendix 11

Re: The Right to Stay Put (Section Six):

The Tryweryn Dam

In September 2005 Liverpool Council apologised on behalf of the city for the distress it caused in the 1960s when it flooded a valley in North Wales to provide its citizens with water

A village of some 60 people and farmhouses was compulsorily purchased after an Act of Parliament was passed, supported by English MPs and opposed by Welsh MPs. The valley and a way of life went under the water. The anger generated is said to have helped to boost the Welsh nationalist political party, Plaid Cymru, and to spark more militant actions.

With the 'Right to Stay Put' a vote in Parliament could still have been decisive. But the process and outcomes could have been very different.

Liverpool Council could not have deceived the valley people as to its intentions. Its initial surveys pretended to an interest in the mineral deposits. It could not have got away with the bare and mean market value compensations. The value of the water to the city would have been openly judged against the value of land and livelihoods.

The dispossessed have been marked for life, it seems. And the new generation marked by their elders' losses and their own. They have difficulty finding the words, in some instances; they talk of being robbed, but of more than their properties and places. What exactly was stolen?

To get their water the big people taught the little people a lesson. A Right to Stay Put would have the big people coming cap in hand. The little people teaching the lesson.

Appendix 12

Poem by Mike Perrett Ashton Vale, Bristol

This Poem Is Written In Conjunction With The P. P. G.
Of Observation Taken From The Bristol Prefab Sites

Reflections As Seen Through
The Eyes Of A Pensioner

My neighbour tells me that the Council wants our ground
My Prefabs on the level, makes it easier to get around
Pensioners in their eighties, one aged ninety two
Talking to each other what are we going to do

To care for us in our twilight years it really is a must
But we've had so many broken promises, we don't know who
to trust

We went to all the meetings, it made us all depressed
Some Tenants now are moving out what happens to the rest
A neighbour is in a bad way, confined to a wheelchair
To give the likes of us the worry, does the Council even care
My neighbour has filled out a transfer form, how I wish it were
not true
She's been so kind and helpful especially when I've had flu

This arthritis gets no better in my legs and aching back
No good the Council offering me a sixth floor high rise flat
There's a neighbour with a white stick that he uses so he can
see
All day long he worries and cannot sleep, just like you and me
Another has angina made worse with all the trouble
He fears he will have a heart attack, if his Prefabs turned to
rubble
My garden I've looked after all these many years
The very thought of leaving it brings on floods of tears
No one wants to listen now we are old and turned to grey
But we're hoping for a miracle, praying we can stay.

POEMS BY JACQUI HANDLEY, NEWPORT

A Tribute to Mabel

Why do they tell me I have to move
I'm getting older and I'm a little confused
My zimmer helps me get around
To bathroom to kitchen and into the lounge
I know my way around this place
But it will be gone and leave no trace
They are pulling the prefabs down
All over Newport town
I'm a little confused
Will there be room to put all my things
Mother's sideboard and sentimental rings
Knick knacks the children won at the fair
It might only be a prefab but it's my home
Why don't they leave me alone
I'm a little confused

My friends and neighbours know where I am
Will they still pass by me
I do hope they can
Oh please tell me soon
What is your plan
I'm thinking these things
I live on a corner and it's easy you see
They have to pass by and
They share a thought for me,
Will they forget me when they don't have to pass my door
I need the answer or I'll just worry more
I'm a little confused

When I'm in my bed and sleep doesn't come
I worry the papers, the papers lots come every day
Lots of words I see
But no understanding for people like me
I hope that they leave me just where I am
And hope that I'm not involved in their plan.

Time's Moving On

Memories
Can I wrap them in soft tissue paper so they don't break
Can I box them up
Can I take them all with me.
Will I still remember
When I don't still hear my creaking floorboard
Nor my gate, which gently creaks
Or my dripping tap that helps me sleep
They will all be gone
Today, I will move.

I dread the knock at my door
When they come to take me
To where I've not been before
Fox the movers will put my home into boxes
Where will I be
Will I still be here or will I be over there
All I know there's no one to really care.
They try to tell me that all will be fine
But that still doesn't settle my minds
Oh dear did they dig up the gladioli that stand so tall
I cut them in the summer and place them in a vase in the hall
Oh dear did they tell the milkman I do hope he knows what to do.
He always come and collects his money at two
And I'll be gone.
My old tabby cat knows something is wrong
And barely raises his eyelids as if to shut it all out
I am so glad he doesn't know what it's all about.
I look around then close my eyes tightly
I make a mental picture of everything I see
So that I can take that picture with me
You see
My home has meant the world to me.
Times running on now not long to go
I've tried to cope
But I know when the door knocker hits the metal door
This will not be my home anymore.

Acknowledgements

With special thanks to Betty King, Shirley Sansom
Margaret Jones, Kate Dumbleton, Stan Dumbleton,
Dave and Jane Drew

Printed in the United Kingdom
by Lightning Source UK Ltd.
118828UK00001B/307-342